NON-STOP PEEPSHOW

Famed Windmill Theater which never closed during war presenting never-clothed girls displays nudes in dignified fashion which does not embarrass stiff upper lip of even straight-laced Britons.

LINED UP at entrance to London's Windmill Theater, in the heart of city's naughty Soho square mile, peepshow fans wait patiently for box office to open. Once inside they will be treated to pretty girls doing versions of the can can (left), fan dances and various nude tableaux.

By Graham Fisher

BACK in the days when the 16th Century huntsmen of merrie England gave out with a shrill cry of "So-ho!" as they pursued the fox across the open fields which are now London's West End, a windmill stood nearby, its sails revolving steadily as it ground the corn harvested by local farmers. The district has seen quite a few changes since then. Open fields have given way to brightly-lit shops, movie houses, and the statue of Eros points his arrow at the prostitutes who ply their trade round Piccadilly Circus. The old hunting cry has given its name to Soho, that cosmopolitan area of narrow back-streets, late-night eating places and dingy night clubs which is London's naughty square mile. Where the windmill stood there now stands the Windmill Theater, its leg shows going round and round with the same regularity as the sails of the old mill—"still grinding out corn," say unkind critics—but at considerably more profit.

In recent years this peepshow of a theater has become one of the most lucrative entertainment palaces in London. Though it seats only 320 people, its non-stop routine of six shows a day enables it to play to an average of 360,000 people a year who push something like $660,000 through

Striptease

Strip

tease

from GASLIGHT to SPOTLIGHT

Jessica Glasscock

HARRY N. ABRAMS, INC., PUBLISHERS

To my husband Dennis, who now realizes that there is such a thing as knowing too much about striptease.

Contents

Introduction

The 1950s stripteaser is a uniquely American icon. She is pink, well fed, and smiling, with tassel-tipped breasts that sparkle like the chrome detailing on a classic car. Looking at pictures of the striptease stars of a half-century ago, one can only conclude that they don't make them like that anymore. Although stripping still

exists today—and is big business—
the 1950s nightclub stage act known
as the striptease faded from popularity in the 1960s. What went with it
was the culmination and distillation
of almost a century of provocative
performance by women willing to
show anything from a little leg to a
spectacular pair of breasts.

IT IS THE HISTORY OF THE CLASSIC STRIPTEASE THAT THIS book proposes to relate—a history that intersects with the development of popular theater, the coded eroticism of nineteenth-century academic art, the march of imperialism, the advent of consumerism, and the triumph of mass production in America. It is also a history that creates a window into American culture that is beyond the generalities of "prudish" gilded-age parlors and the "roaring" liberation of the 1920s. It is a story of undercurrents, underclasses, and underwear. And it is a history of undeniable fun aimed not at the head, the heart, or even the stomach, but just south of all three.

The logical starting point for such a history is a definition of the word *striptease*. The striptease has taken as many forms as it has had performers, but it has always been characterized by four essential actions: revealing, arousing, amusing, and doing all of these on a stage (although not necessarily in that order). Revealing entails that at some point in the act the audience gets to see more. What constitutes "more" and how much more the audience gets to see has changed over time. But it is always something: an ankle, an upper thigh, an ass cheek, or even a glimpse of genitalia. Arousing is a more enigmatic act . . . or perhaps just a more inarticulable one. If a striptease is properly executed, the response is physical. If it isn't, the stripteaser is doing something wrong. But the striptease has to be more than just sexually exciting, it also has to be entertaining. It has to make the audience smile or laugh or gasp. It is this emphasis on providing the audience with some amusement—a shtick of some kind—that differentiates the striptease from the mere stripping off of clothes. The final necessity of

a good striptease is in the nature of the relationship of the audience to the performer. A real striptease is a stage act. It requires a certain amount of distance between the teaser and the teasee—a distance that makes the tease possible by allowing the audience members to return home, morals relatively intact. The combination of all these elements defines striptease.

The best and brightest of the stripteasers provided all four in perfect concert. Seminal 1930s stripteaser Gypsy Rose Lee—known as much for her wit as her shapely legs—ascended to national celebrity with an act that was a combination comedy monologue and girlie show. 1950s stripteaser Lili St. Cyr became a top Vegas draw by making use of both her meticulously maintained body and elaborate sets and costumes. New Orleans's top stripteaser Blaze Starr made her name known across the country as much with her red-hot country bumpkin stage patter as her DD-cup breasts.

The variations on the striptease are endless. It can be a belly dance where the dancer rolls her hips in circles as she takes off ever smaller and sheerer harem veils. It may be a fan dance where the performer wears only bra and briefs (or pasties and g-string) and covers and uncovers herself with large feather fans as she dances. Or a bubble dance, similar to the fan dance except that a large, inflated ball is used in place of the fans. It can be a "reverse strip" where the performer starts out in silk pajamas and gets dressed on the stage, showing off legs and bosom in the process. It might be a bump and grind act where the dancer, accompanied by a live band, strips down to tasseled pasties and a fringed g-string and performs dance moves that cause the

A 1950S STRIPTEASE IN PROGRESS. *Jada* IS THE UNHOLY ALLIANCE OF ZIEGFELD SHOWGIRL, ZAFTIG NINETEENTH-CENTURY BURLESQUE QUEEN, "EXOTIC" CARNIVAL DANCER, AND OLD-TIME VAUDEVILLIAN. ALL OF THESE CHARACTERS WERE EARLY PROTOTYPES FOR LATTER-DAY STRIPTEASERS.

A PICTURE IS WORTH A THOUSAND WORDS—PARTICULARLY AS IT COULD BE USED TO DEFEND STRIPTEASE PERFORMERS AGAINST OBSCENITY CHARGES.
THE RELATIONSHIP BETWEEN STRIPTEASE AND HIGH ART IS LONG AND COMPLEX. THE EARLIEST NUDE PERFORMERS ON THE STAGE WERE PRESENTED
AS PURELY EDUCATIONAL PARTICIPANTS IN TABLEAUX VIVANTS—LIVING PICTURES INTENDED TO EVOKE GREAT WORKS OF ART. IF IT WAS ART, OF COURSE,
IT COULDN'T BE OBSCENE—OR LEGALLY ACTIONABLE AS SUCH. CONSEQUENTLY, "LIVING" STATUARY, SETS DESIGNED TO LOOK LIKE FRAMES, AND
FAVORITE CLASSICAL SUBJECTS SUCH AS NYMPHS ARE PERVASIVE IN THE HISTORY OF STRIPTEASE.

62

Pauline Markham WAS VENUS IN FURS AS FAR AS THE MEN IN AMERICAN THEATRICAL AUDIENCES OF THE 1870S WERE CONCERNED. SHE, ALONGSIDE HER TROUPE LEADER LYDIA THOMPSON, WAS ONE OF THE FIRST BIG DRAWS OF THE BURLESQUE HOUSES WHERE STRIPTEASE WOULD BE BORN. ALTHOUGH BEAUTY STANDARDS WOULD SHIFT OVER TIME, MARKHAM, WITH HER PRONOUNCED FEMININE FORM, SET THE ORIGINAL SEX QUEEN PROTOTYPE ON THE AMERICAN STAGE. THE KEY TO HER APPEAL (AND THE SCANDAL OF NINE-TEENTH-CENTURY BURLESQUE) WAS HER LEGS, A PART OF THE FEMALE BODY THAT WAS OTHERWISE UNKNOWN IN PUBLIC LIFE.

tassels and fringe to shimmy and shake. Or it may be a comedy act where the stripteaser jokes with, mocks, and taunts the audience as she rips away a sequined outfit. It can, at its simplest, be a pretty girl in a pretty dress . . . and then not. If the audience gets to take a peek and come away satisfied, it is a *striptease.*

The striptease did not spring whole from the mind of some red-blooded American boy with money from his paper route and a taste for tassels. It has a history. But finding that history is a difficult task. No school of dance is willing to take credit for the invention of the bump or the grind. There are no stage directions for a fan dance or a reverse strip in any script on record. The origins of

the word *striptease* can be traced to the 1920s, but the act already existed at that time, and had for many years before. The question remains, where did it begin? Most theater historians have answered by placing the origins of striptease in the nineteenth-century theatrical form known as burlesque. In Robert C. Allen's exhaustively researched history of the subject, *Horrible Prettiness,* the development of burlesque in America follows a trajectory beginning with nineteenth-century comic plays that featured cross-dressed girls doing high kicks up through to the outlaw entertainment of the 1930s that was centered around blue comedy, bawdy production numbers, and striptease performances. That view of striptease's inception explains the irrevocable association between the word *burlesque* and the striptease that is still prevalent today. But that explanation does not account for all that is striptease. The fan dance did not come out of a burlesque theater. Nor did the idea of an "exotic" dance that many early stripteasers used to frame their acts. The striptease is more than just a burlesque performance, and a closer examination reveals that its origins lie in other forms of American theater as well. Elements of the striptease were drawn from modern dance, vaudeville, variety shows, and Broadway revues. This is a fact that has been obscured by most histories of these forms, however, as historians of vaudeville and even burlesque have minimized the connection between those forms and the striptease; while the chroniclers of modern dance and Broadway revues have ignored it almost completely.

In his 1953 book *Vaudeville: From Honky-tonks to the Palace,* vaudeville historian Joe Laurie Jr. states that "strip-tease dancing . . . never belonged or ever got in vaudeville, thank God!" His version of vaudeville history posits a sexually innocuous form of entertainment, where all female performers lie well within the bounds of decency. In almost the same breath, however, he revels in salacious descriptions of the bathing beauties, skirt dancers, and other early stage femme fatales who drew male audiences to vaudeville. Between the lines of his tale, a prurient interest in certain vaudeville acts is easily discerned and therein lies a significant piece of the history of striptease. Although the vaudeville women of Laurie's book were not performing stripteases a 1950s audience would have recognized, their acts had the same elements and the same purpose.

Burlesque historian Bernard Sobel is equally dismissive of striptease in his narrative. He remarks

Anna Held NEVER STRIPPED, BUT SHE WAS CONSIDERED A SEX-POT ICON BY LATE-NINETEENTH-CENTURY STANDARDS. SHE HAD BIG, BEAUTIFUL EYES THAT WERE THE SUBJECT OF HER SIGNATURE SONG ("I CAN'T MAKE MY EYES BEHAVE") WHEN FLORENZ ZIEGFELD JR. "DISCOVERED" HER IN THE MUSIC HALLS OF PARIS. IN AMERICA, SHE WOULD STAR IN SEVERAL MUSICAL COMEDIES THAT WOULD LAUNCH ZIEGFELD AS A BROADWAY PRODUCER SPECIALIZING IN PRESENTING BEAUTIFUL WOMEN IN BEAUTIFUL CLOTHES THAT MORE OR LESS COVERED THEIR BEAUTIFUL BODIES. ALTHOUGH NEVER SO SCANDALOUS THAT SHE RAN AFOUL OF THE LAW, HELD DID ESTABLISH HERSELF AS A STRIPTEASE PRECURSOR BY PERFORMING A "QUICK CHANGE" IN ONE PLAY, CHANGING DRESSES BEHIND A "SCREEN" OF CHORUS GIRLS. IT WAS THE SUGGESTION OF NUDITY BY PERFORMERS LIKE HELD THAT MADE ITS ACTUALITY POSSIBLE DECADES LATER.

opposite: THE HIGH LIFE OF A DIRTY OLD MAN IN TURN-OF-THE-CENTURY NEW YORK CITY WAS EPITOMIZED BY THE CONSUMPTION OF CHAMPAGNE, LOBSTER, AND CHORUS GIRLS. PATRONAGE BY THE RICH AND POWERFUL WAS A STAPLE OF PUBLICITY FOR BURLESQUE QUEENS, ZIEGFELD GIRLS, MINSKY STRIPTEASERS, AND PLAYBOY BUNNIES. THE SURFEIT OF WEALTHY MALE FANS WITH OPEN WALLETS WAS ONE OF THE FAVORITE MYTHS OF SHOWGIRL LIFESTYLE, WHETHER OR NOT IT WAS BASED IN FACT.

365 DAYS AHEAD OF THEM ALL
BON-TON
BURLESQUERS
"A WARM RECEPTION"

in his 1956 book *A Pictorial History of Burlesque* that, "The fatal force [against burlesque] was striptease." Sobel's position is that "real" burlesque had been bawdy, satirical plays that were at first enlivened and then insidiously destroyed by the presence of women whose sex appeal became the center of the show. Although women, and more specifically women's legs, had always been at the heart of burlesque shows, Sobel de-emphasizes female stars in favor of male comic "geniuses." When he does acknowledge the women of early burlesque, it is only to contrast real burlesque with the appalling state of 1950s striptease. In case his point should be missed, he provides several pictures of the offending women.

No longer living and viable forms of theater in the 1950s, vaudeville and burlesque were essentially being eulogized by Laurie and Sobel. In their work, they hoped to raise the cultural stock of these forms of popular theater that had been otherwise ignored in the history of the American stage. The striptease, known to the 1950s audience as a risqué and possibly seedy enterprise, needed to be disinherited so that the association would not taint vaudeville and burlesque. But their agenda is transparent and ultimately the fact that all of the elements of striptease were present in the ostensibly "innocent" acts of the nineteenth-century stage titillation described by historians cannot be hidden. The fundamentals of striptease—revealing, arousing, and amusing—were an integral part of women's performance in the nineteenth-and early-twentieth-century popular theater.

What aids Laurie and Sobel in their act of concealment, and further complicates the connection between popular theater and the striptease, is the shifting standard of decency between the 1860s, when burlesque hit the American stage in its early

form, and the 1950s, when striptease was ascendant. Even if one wanted to find the connection rather than hide it, how does one equate the shimmying, g-string wearing entertainer letting it all hang out to the woman performing a slow dance in a long skirt revealing her ankles? The answer becomes clearer after reading a controversial 1891 Minnesota state senate bill. It proposed:

> That any female who shall, upon the stage or platform in any theatre or opera house, concert hall, or any public space whatever, where other persons are present, expose her nether limb or limbs dressed in tights, so called, or in any manner whatever so that the shape and form of her nether limb or limbs are plainly visible to such other persons present, shall be guilty of open and gross lewdness, and lascivious behavior, and guilty of a misdemeanor, and upon conviction thereof shall be punished by a fine of not less than $5 nor more than $100, or imprisonment in the county jail not less than five days nor more than thirty.

Clearly, the bar for shocking behavior was considerably lower during the late nineteenth century (at least in Minnesota). Although it has already been established that women's legs were hardly unknown on the Victorian stage and that, in fact, they were the main source of the appeal of early burlesque shows and the primary selling point for vaudeville performers who were advertised as "skirt dancers," it still remains that the sight of a woman's "nether limbs" on a stage was not universally accepted. If you wanted to get rid of them, you had to legislate against them. Which they did. Although, not to much effect. And, much to the chagrin of the nineteenth-century censor, women's "nether limbs" were not the only cause for concern. The standards of

THE TIGHTS WORN BY EARLY
BURLESQUE QUEENS EVOLVED
INTO SCANDALOUS "FLESHINGS,"
FULL-BODY STOCKINGS WORN
WITHOUT A CORSET.

GG
Cº

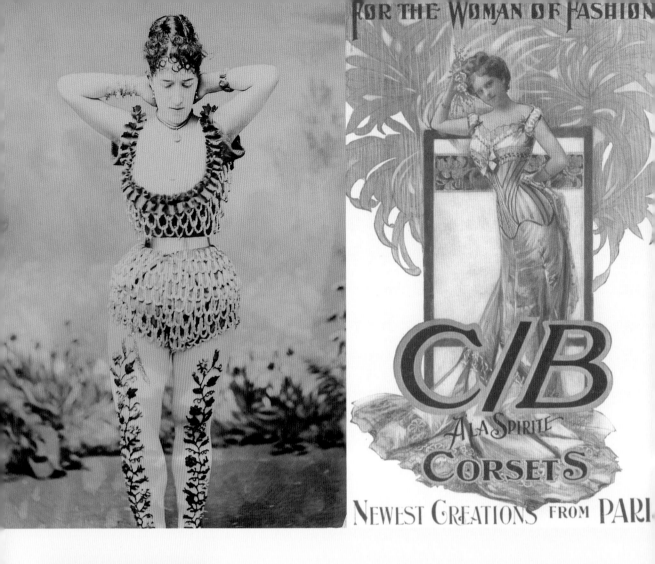

top left: AS THE ENTERTAINMENT KNOWN AS BURLESQUE BECAME MORE AND MORE CONCENTRATED ON WOMEN IN CORSETS AND TIGHTS, THE CORSETS AND TIGHTS BECAME MORE AND MORE ATTENTION GETTING.

top right: IN THE NINETEENTH CENTURY, THE CORSET WAS MORE THAN JUST LINGERIE, IT WAS THE FOUNDATION OF WESTERN WOMANHOOD. IT SEPARATED DECENT WOMEN FROM PROSTITUTES AND CULTURED SOCIETY MEMBERS FROM PRIMITIVE HEATHENS. A LADY OF THE NINETEENTH CENTURY ONLY REMOVED HER CORSET IN THE MOST INTIMATE SITUATION. A WOMAN WHO WALKED ON STAGE WITHOUT ONE WAS PERCEIVED TO BE GIVING MEN AN OPEN INVITATION INTO HER BEDROOM.

left: FLESHINGS ARE USED HERE TO DRESS THE "ARTISTIC" NUDE OF THE TABLEAU VIVANT. LIVING STATUARY SUCH AS THESE WERE A POPULAR ATTRACTION FOR THE WHOLE FAMILY AT CIRCUSES, DIME MUSEUMS, AND VAUDEVILLE HOUSES IN THE LATE 1890S. MOTHER AND CHILDREN COULD ENJOY AN ART HISTORY LESSON WHILE FATHER MIGHT CONSIDER SOME OF THE OTHER IMPLICATIONS OF THREE WOMEN EMBRACING.

decency in the nineteenth and early twentieth centuries were such that revealing in order to arouse and amuse didn't even require showing an inch of bare skin.

The corset was part of the standard of sartorial decency in the nineteenth century. From the 1830s to 1910, it was the basic undergarment worn by most women, the foundation to decent dress because it kept a woman "composed." It was so integral to women's dress that even the women of burlesque who cross-dressed for men's roles wore corsets underneath and had their costumes fashioned to them. This was essentially how they were able to get away with revealing their stocking-clad legs; once the audience had recovered from the presumable shock of the exposed thigh, they could take comfort in the corset. Without it, the early burlesque woman would have *really* been undressed. For nineteenth- and early-twentieth-century performers brave enough to transgress the standard of the corset, there was the full-body stocking known as *fleshings.* These were knitted garments that covered the wearer's whole body from ankles to wrists. They were generally flesh colored or white to create the illusion of nudity. And, actually, the nudity wasn't an illusion to their audience since it had been functionally achieved with the removal of the corset. Fleshings were worn by performers who stood motionless in imitation of Greek statues. They were also used to fill the role of nudity in the soft-core pornography of the nineteenth century—covertly distributed photographs of some of the more scandalous nineteenth-century dancers that had fleshings seam lines retouched into nonexistence so as to suggest full nudity. They were worn under costumes that were translucent, leaving the body exposed even as it was completely encased in fabric. They were the

base on which rhinestones, flowers, and other strategically placed decorations were sewn so that audience members might think the performers were wearing nothing but the rhinestones or flowers. Fleshings were the illusion of nudity in which the audience willingly participated.

Performing in tights or without corsets or in fleshings was common in vaudeville and burlesque and was a cause of great concern for self-appointed and government censors of the day. It is within these wholly different standards of what qualified a woman as "dressed" in the nineteenth and early twentieth centuries that the precursors to the striptease are hidden. How much was hidden illuminates how much was being revealed—and how the revelation was intended. Without an understanding of what scandalized and titillated Victorian audiences, historians of theater could easily dismiss any connection with striptease as they compare hazy, nostalgic memories of sex symbols past with more confrontational versions of the present. The image of a nineteenth-century skirt dancer who was only swishing her skirt and gently lifting her leg in time to a waltz is soothing indeed until one considers that women's ankles weren't even seen at the time and that men were attending performances with the specific hope that they would get the chance to see her unmentionables. The history of striptease examined in this context provides a much richer story than has yet been told. Instead of being a fringe element in the history of American theater, striptease is exposed as part of the mainstream. The striptease act—revealing, arousing, and amusing—has never been fully outlawed or fully censored. It has only gone unacknowledged and unnamed. ✩

IN THE BEGINNING...

or

THOSE PRUDISH VICTORIANS

opposite: VICTORIAN SKIRT DANCER *Mabel Clark* OVERDOING IT WITH THE LACE TRIM.

Addie Conyers WAS ONE OF SEVERAL AMERICAN ANSWERS TO LYDIA THOMPSON WHO TOURED ON THE NINETEENTH-CENTURY BURLESQUE CIRCUIT.

Probably the pictorial exhibition of the shameless woman on the New-York [sic] theatrical stage was never bolder or more common than it is in this hour when a civilized community might be expected to have no humor for trifling, and to take life seriously. . . . To denounce these performers by name is merely to advertise them. They want to be denounced. No one knows better than they, except their managers, that they have abandoned all right to respect and are devoid of all that is charming in womanhood. Audacity is their only gift; notoriety is necessary to their existence.

—From the *New York Times* editorial page, September 11, 1892

THE SUPPOSEDLY BUTTONED-DOWN VICTORIANS LAID THE foundation for the invention of striptease before 1900. They were fully aware of the concept of sex appeal, even if they were not entirely approving of it. By the middle of the nineteenth century, the sex appeal of the dramatic stage actress was an important marketing strategy. Performers' reputations for supplementing their earnings with the "protection" of wealthy men were publicized by theatrical promoters as additional proof of their desirability. The ostensible promiscuity of the performer provided an added source of titillation for an audience eager to equate female stage performer with readily available sex object. Once this correspondence had been established, the mere act of mounting a public stage could constitute a shameless exhibition—one that would be profitably exploited in all sorts of entertainment venues in nineteenth-century America.

Although many venues used sex appeal to sell tickets, American concert saloons pioneered the art of using sex appeal to sell alcohol. Concert saloons were large spaces that featured strong drink, gambling, and waitresses in short dresses. They appeared in the 1850s in response to a transition in American theater—the dirty, rowdy, and vocal pit audience was replaced by a more reserved, middle-class dominated audience—and the displaced, catcalling working-class theatergoers moved to the saloons. The concert saloons, also called honky-tonks and free-and-easies, opened in cities across the United States, particularly in New York and the gold rush towns of the West where working men with surplus cash were in need of entertainment. Owners of the saloons didn't pay the first entertainers at all: these minstrel shows were performed only for throw money. Since saloon owners saw an increase in alcohol

sales as a result of those shows, they added stages to their spaces to accommodate them and sometimes took on a "management" role, which enabled them to demand a cut of performers' profits. Once the stage was built, other variety performers appeared: singers, dancers, two-man acts, sister acts, family acts, jugglers, strong men, contortionists, Irish comedians, German comedians, Jewish comedians, blackface comedians, performers in silent spectacles such as tableaux vivants, and various freak acts such as dwarfs, giants, and bearded ladies. Also, in an innovation that has been retained in modern striptease venues, saloon owners encouraged the skimpy-skirted waitresses and hostesses to persuade the customers to buy *them* drinks, giving the women a kickback for the drinks sold. This scheme was improved upon when, according to vaudeville historian Joe Laurie Jr.:

> To make the girls more attractive to the "Johns,"
> the management had them open the show with
> a song and a simple dance. They dressed in
> soubrette costumes, short skirts and low necks.
> This, of course, made them actresses and more
> desirable to the Johns. Some of the girls would
> take turns doing a single and would get throw
> money, adding to their commissions.
>
> The gals soon got wise that they could make
> more and easier money while singing than by sitting with the Johns all night guzzling bad tea and
> worse booze and getting pawed. Their percentage
> on drinks was small . . . . They started telling their
> friends not to spend their dough on booze for
> them but to throw the money to them when they
> were on the stage singing. . . .
>
> It didn't take long for the owners to get wise to
> what was going on. They passed a rule that it was
> unladylike and unprofessional to have performers

pick up the throw money, so to save embarrassment *they* would pick it up and give the girls 20 per cent of the take. That ended one of the first theatrical rackets and turned saloonkeepers into managers!

Although concert saloons flourished in the 1870s and 1880s and became the training ground for performers of vaudeville and the legitimate stage, some of the denizens of nineteenth-century America could not tolerate entertainment in the morally dubious venue of the saloon. Women in particular were late to be won over by the enticements of these popular entertainment spots. Understandably, middle-class women did not want to be in a place where they could be mistaken for hostesses who were associated in the middle-class mind with prostitutes. Women (and their children) would need other inducements to consider being entertained—inducements that the growing entertainment industry in America was eager to identify in order to continue expanding. So, a woman's place was designated: the American dime museum.

Originally the noble experiment of painter and naturalist Charles Wilson Peale, the first dime museum was founded in Philadelphia in 1784. Its initial purpose was to provide scholarly exhibits of paintings and natural curiosities. As a result of the early success of Peale's museum, others were founded across America. By the early 1800s, scholarly exhibits began to lose hold on consumer interest, particularly when compared to the delights of the theater and the circus, which were quickly gaining popularity. Driven by the necessity of turning a profit, museums began to offer lectures by "professors" who were more likely to be trained on the carnival midway than in the ivy-covered halls of academia. These speakers did whatever it took

IN AMERICAN VARIETY HOUSES, BALLET DANCERS WERE ENCOURAGED TO SHOW OFF A LITTLE LEG IN THE NAME OF HIGH ART.

to draw a crowd and were as likely to offer a lecture on temperance as they were to moderate a question-and-answer session with President George Washington's 150-year-old nurse. The museums also made use of sensationalistic oddities, such as P. T. Barnum's "Fejee Mermaid," a desiccated monkey torso seamlessly attached to a similarly preserved fish tail that attracted thousands who wanted to see just how unreal it was. As museums were pressed to bring in more customers, they also expanded into "moral and instructional" plays presented on the lecturer's stage. One early hit on the dime museum stage was *The Drunkard,* a temperance drama that used the still extant formula of reveling in bad behavior before concluding the tale with crushing consequences to the wrongdoer.

ACCORDING TO NINETEENTH-CENTURY MORAL
STANDARDS, THE IDEA THAT A DANCER WAS
PORTRAYING A BIRD WAS AS GOOD AN EXCUSE
AS ANY TO GET HER SKIRT OFF.

Niblo's Garden WAS ONE OF AMERICA'S FIRST GREAT THEATERS. IT WAS KNOWN NOT FOR SHAKESPEARE, BUT FOR SPECTACLES AND EXTRAVAGANZAS THAT FEATURED LARGE CASTS OF BEAUTIFUL CHORUS GIRLS. EQUIPPED TO HANDLE COMPLEX SETS AND EFFECTS, IT HOSTED THE PREMIERE OF THE SPECTACULAR *The Black Crook* AND LYDIA THOMPSON'S SECOND BURLESQUE, *The Forty Thieves.*

Wood's Museum WAS A DIME MUSEUM ON A GRAND SCALE, MUCH LIKE P. T. BARNUM'S AMERICAN MUSEUM. ALTHOUGH DIME MUSEUM PERFORMANCES WERE SUPPOSED TO BE IN SOME WAY EDUCATIONAL, WOOD'S OPENING FEATURED LYDIA THOMPSON AND HER BRITISH BLONDES. CRITICS SUGGESTED THAT PERHAPS THE SHOW WAS INTENDED AS A LESSON ON THE ANATOMY OF THE FEMALE LEG.

These melodramas alongside human freaks, gory waxworks, flea circuses, rough slapstick comedy, and body-baring "demonstrations" of skirt dancing characterized dime museums by the 1880s. Considered suitable for ladies, they were also the primary entertainment for urban, immigrant families. As American entertainment developed in the nineteenth century, the dime museum would ultimately present acts barely distinguishable from those that played on the vaudeville, variety, and burlesque stages.

All of the venues available for nineteenth-century entertainment held some moral pitfalls. The entertainers of the dramatic stage were of questionable virtue. The stages of the concert saloons were rife with overly friendly barmaids. The dime museums were baldly hypocritical. And it was in this cultural climate that what was called *burlesque* appeared in the form of Lydia Thompson and her British Blondes. The troupe premiered in New York

City in 1868 at Wood's Broadway Theatre. Their play, *Ixion,* was a satirical take on classical themes and featured popular songs of the day, bad puns, sexual innuendoes, performers who directly addressed the audience, women in breeches (performing men's roles), and a chorus line of peroxided dancers in short breeches or slit skirts revealing legs encased only in flesh-colored tights. At the end of the show, the women lined up and kicked their legs in unison. Audiences were alternately thrilled and appalled.

Beyond the novelty of the massive, quivering thighs that shook the stage and apparently the audience at Wood's Broadway Theatre, the theatrical form that Lydia Thompson had created in *Ixion* was not entirely original. The idea of women in "breeches" roles (as well as the popular songs, bad puns, and sexual innuendoes) came from the music halls of England, where first men and then women cross-dressed for comical and satirical effect. Even earlier breeches roles had a theatrical precedent in

Lydia Thompson WAS THE ORIGI-
NAL QUEEN OF BURLESQUE. SHE
PREMIERED WITH HER TROUPE IN
THE UNITED STATES IN 1867 AND
PERFORMED AROUND THE COUNTRY
UNTIL THE END OF THE NINETEENTH
CENTURY. SHE WAS ALSO ONE OF
THE FIRST MODERN CELEBRITIES,
ARRIVING ON THE SCENE JUST AS
THE MASS PRODUCTION OF PHOTO-
GRAPHIC IMAGES HAD BEEN PER-
FECTED. THOMPSON'S STATUS AS A
STAR GOES A LONG WAY TOWARD
EXPLAINING THE APPEAL OF THE
DISREPUTABLE GENRE OF BUR-
LESQUE TO YOUNG AMERICAN GIRLS
WHO WANTED TO GO ON STAGE.

THE FAMOUS RENTZ SANTLEY NOVELTY & BURLESQUE
COMPANY WAS THE FIRST BURLESQUE COMPANY FOUNDED
BY AN AMERICAN. THE BRAINCHILD OF IMPRESARIO
MICHAEL LEAVITT, THE COMPANY PRESENTED THE WHOLE
GAMUT OF NINETEENTH-CENTURY AMERICAN BURLESQUE
FROM THE RAGE FOR BRITISH BLONDE COMEDIENNES TO
THE LATER ADORATION OF CANCAN DANCERS. THIS POSTER
FROM THE 1890S SHOWS HOW BURLESQUE AT THE END OF
THE NINETEENTH CENTURY WAS STARTING TO MEAN "GIRLS,
GIRLS, GIRLS" RATHER THAN GIRLS DRESSED AS BOYS.

SOME OF BURLESQUE'S SEEDY REPUTATION WAS OF ITS OWN
MAKING. MARKETING FOR DEVERE'S HIGH ROLLERS BURLESQUE
COMPANY MADE A PARTICULAR FETISH OF THE LOW MORAL
CHARACTER OF ITS CHORUS GIRLS.

IN 1860S AND 1870S AMERICAN POPULAR THEATER, YOU COULDN'T
BE TOO BRITISH OR TOO BLONDE. THIS POSTER IS FROM THAT
PERIOD, CONSIDERED THE HEYDAY OF BURLESQUE BY HISTORIANS
OF THE GENRE.

the plays of William Shakespeare, among others.
Ixion's satire of classical themes also had a long
history in traditional theater and was familiar to
Americans as an element of minstrelsy performance. Tights had been worn by women performing
as ballerinas, in equestrian spectacles, and most
notoriously in music hall and American concert
saloon entertainments in performances known
as *tableaux vivants,* wherein a woman appeared
(sometimes behind a fabric screen lit from behind)
dressed only in a flesh-colored body stocking,
striking the pose of a classical artwork. But it was
the effect of all of these elements combined with
exuberant high kicking that was stunning to
the American theater-going public.

Lydia Thompson's performance also marked the
first appearance of a mass-consumable sex symbol
in American culture, as evidenced by the numerous
collectible cabinet photos of her and of the women
in her troupe. Thompson and her troupe were
showered with critical praise and had tremendous
financial success on their first outing in New York.
In later productions, however, a backlash ensued.
Clergymen, editorialists, and feminists expressed
their strong moral concerns. Theatrical critics who
were initially enthusiastic cooled considerably.
The "decency" of the costumes and tights was ques-
tioned. In an era where men and women's dress was
unquestioningly differentiated and women's legs
were never revealed, the costumes were considered

overly provocative. Never mind theater, prostitution, or fraudulent mermaids, this was an "unnecessary and lewd exhibition of their persons" according to the *Chicago Times.*

Despite the backlash, the money kept coming in for Thompson. She was followed by other troupes of British blondes who were able to cash in as well. Within a few short years of Thompson's premiere, American theater impresario Michael Leavitt was able to create a profitable formula for burlesque that was dispersed throughout the United States by way of touring companies that he established. With Thompson's plays as an inspiration, Leavitt's companies featured male comics, beautiful blondes in tights, and minstrel skits. The structure of his shows was loosely narrative, but Leavitt was not one to spend too much on a writer when a nice pair of legs could distract from any plot insufficiencies. The touring circuit he created blazed a path for other entertainments to make their way across America. Whereas small minstrel troupes had only hoped for throw money, Leavitt's burlesque companies were enough of a draw to demand a set fee from the venue as well as a piece of the box office. The precedent set by burlesque expanded the profit potential of the nation's entertainment industry as a whole. From Leavitt's formula, burlesque in America became associated with both satirical plays and performances that offered a good view of the star and chorus's legs. Elements of Leavitt's version of burlesque spread into all of the American entertainment venues and a circuit of theaters developed that featured burlesques modeled on Lydia Thompson's entertainment.

Developing simultaneously with burlesque was the variety show, a hodgepodge of acts featured in working class theaters, some dime museums, and concert saloons. A variety show was not a play, but a series of acts, some of which featured the same lovely ladies as the burlesque circuit. In a sense, variety was just a burlesque without the pretense of structure (of which burlesque shows had very little themselves, but tried to maintain the illusion of). There were comedians telling jokes, there were popular songs, and there were pretty girls on display. Variety as a theatrical form was the basis for the peculiarly American phenomenon of vaudeville, as well as the Broadway revues of the early twentieth century. As vaudeville became a growing phenomenon toward the end of the nineteenth century, variety continued to exist as a separate, increasingly professionalized form. To the historians of vaudeville, variety also served as a term used to avoid the tainted term *burlesque,* even if the two forms were at times indistinguishable. By the early twentieth century, a lighted marquee announcing "VARIETY" could appear on a burlesque or vaudeville venue, and by the 1950s it was used to describe the vaudeville acts that appeared on early television shows and was fully disassociated with naughty girls in tights.

As burlesques, variety shows, and other entertainments became more profitable in America, popular theater became a more tightly organized entity— like many other American industries in the late nineteenth century. The minstrel comics and singing waitresses of variety professionalized and were, consequently, sanitized by theater managers such as B. F. Keith who ran what was known as the "Sunday school" circuit of theaters. From this process, vaudeville was born. Although the origins of the word *vaudeville* are in dispute, what is certain is that vaudeville was supposed to be "clean." It was created in opposition to burlesque and variety shows, as an entertainment for ladies and children that was without the taint of moral corruption. It

MARCELLA BERG

CORA STRONG

THE TWO FACES OF NINETEENTH-CENTURY BURLESQUE:
JAUNTILY CROSS-DRESSED COMEDIENNE AND BUXOM,
BACKSOME, FLESHY WOMAN IN TIGHTS. NEITHER WAS
CONSIDERED FAMILY FRIENDLY.

VAUDEVILLE WAS FUN FOR THE WHOLE
FAMILY . . . OR ELSE. PERFORMERS
WHO VIOLATED RULES ON LANGUAGE OR
INDECENCY WOULD FIND THEMSELVES
FINED OR BANNED BY MANAGERS. IF
THOSE MANAGERS HAD KNOWN THAT
THE CHILD PERFORMER PICTURED HERE
WOULD GROW UP TO BE STRIPTEASE
STAR *Gypsy Rose Lee*, THEY PROBABLY
WOULD HAVE BANNED HER AS A
PREVENTATIVE MEASURE.

CANTERBURY

VARIETY THEATRE,

632 BROADWAY, between Bleecker & Houston Sts.
Messrs. Hughes & Gregory . Managers | William Scott. . Stage Manager

Programme for this Evening,
PART FIRST.

FEMALE MINSTREL SCENE

Introductory Overture . . . . Prof. Rolenski's Orchestra
Ballad—Take me Home . . . . Miss Nettie Taylor
Ballad—When the Moon in Glory Brightens. . . . . . . Wm. Scott
COMIC DITTY—Up in a Balloon—1st appearance . . . . JOE CHILDS
Ballad—Kiss me and I'll go to Sleep . . . . Miss Maskill
Ballad—Good Bye as the Door . . . . Ed Reeves
COMIC REFRAIN—Rat Catcher's Daughter . . . . . . JIMMY QUINN
ALLEGORICAL FINALE BY THE COMPANY.

OVERTURE . . . . ORCHESTRA

Fancy Dance . . . . Miss J. Turner

Serio-Comic Song, (1st appearance) Miss Ida Wallace

JIMMY QUINN AND HIS BANJO.

Miss Nettie Taylor . . . . In her Vocalizations

CHAMPION CLOG . . . . . JOE CHILDS

Master James in his Wonderful Contortion Act

Gems from the Emerald Isle . . . Mr. M. Gallagher

The Ball Tosser

Messrs. QUINN, CHILDS & SCOTT.

Comic Song, ... Mr. J. Riley

Tableaux

1. THE THREE GRACES,   5. EDWARDS & COLYER.
2. THE GREEK SLAVE,   6. FIGHTING GLADIATORS
3. ITALIAN BRIGANDS,   7. ARTISTS' STUDIO.
4. GAMBRINUS.

Beautiful Vocal Duett . . . Messrs. Reeves & Scott

HOW FAR TO THE NEXT RANCHE,
Messrs. CHILDS & SCOTT.

M. Gallagher, . . . The Fifth Ward Dancing Master

Favorite Selections . . . Miss Ida Wallace

Tableaux

1. BATTLE OF THE AMAZONS,   4. DYING GLADIATOR
2. VENUS & CUPID,   5. THE THREE GRACES.
3. THE ROMAN WARRIORS,   6. ALLEGORICAL TABLEAU

To be followed by the new and laughable Sketch by H. C. Andrews, of

THE PUZZLED DARKEY

POSEY . . . . JIMMY QUINN
Philip James . . . . . . Ed Reeves | Uncle Robert . . . . Joe Childs
Sheriff Grab . . . . . . M. Gallagher | Kitty Henderson . . Miss J. Turner

The performance will conclude with the

BEAUTIFUL STATUARY

1. PACHA, OR LIFE IN THE SERAGLIO,
2. MOTHER TEACHING HER CHILD TO PRAY.
3. AJAX DEFYING THE LIGHTNING,
4. SYLPHS IN THE LAKE,
5. DYING GLADIATOR,
6. CAIN AND ABEL,
7. SCULPTOR'S STUDIO,
8. SLAVE MARKET IN CONSTANTINOPLE

Admission, 25 Cents. | Orchestra Chairs, 50 Cents

LOOK OUT FOR NEW ATTRACTIONS.

was, in short, a marketing ploy. Theatrical impresarios realized they could double their audience if they reassured women (and their husbands and fathers) that the shows were safe for their consumption. The same marketing that had birthed the "educational" stage shows at the dime museums succeeded brilliantly. The only problem was, vaudeville was never all that clean. Its acts were drawn directly from the burlesque and variety shows of the 1870s and 1880s and, although the language was toned down in vaudeville, and the women in tights were excluded, the shows were very much like variety shows. And the women in tights were not much missed since other titillating women had great success on the vaudeville stage. These performers had been morally legitimized by virtue of importation from Europe where there was less pressure to segregate popular theater into the naughty and the nice. They were known in America as skirt dancers and in the course of their energetic, acrobatic performances, they showed as much leg as the burlesque woman and sometimes more.

In America, the term *skirt dancer* encompassed several distinct dances including the cancan, Spanish dance (generally a fandango or a flamenco), and the serpentine dance. Essentially, any female dancer who was not a ballerina was called a skirt dancer. Of the multiple forms of skirt dance, the first to come to the stage was the one performed by Kate Vaughan. Vaughan was a music hall performer with some ballet training who came to prominence at London's Gaiety Theatre in 1873 when she rejected the traditional tutu and danced instead in long black skirts with a contrasting petticoat and tights spangled with gold. Her dance, which consisted of ballet steps and clog dancing steps and the swishing of her aforementioned skirts, was a sensation and became the premier

attraction of the Gaiety. In 1888, it was introduced to American audiences by touring Gaiety dancers Lettie Lind and Sylvia Grey. This British version of the skirt dance was fairly tame and subdued (especially in contrast to the kicks of the American burlesque queens), involving only the lifting of the leg to waltz tunes. The petticoats, and of course the omnipresent tights, were revealed, but not by much. It was mainly a matter of well-formed ankles. In this way, the Gaiety skirt dance alluded to the sexually suggestive without actually offending the audience. However, as practitioners of the dance toured America, flashes of underclothes became a more common element of the dance as a little peek-a-boo was a sure way to get a cheer from audiences.

The cancan was a skirt dance developing in Paris simultaneously with the British skirt dance, but not as a stage performance. In Parisian dancing gardens in the 1830s, the cancan was a popular social dance. Between the 1840s and 1860s, solo performers of the cancan became a draw at dance halls and the fancy dress balls of France's Second Empire, even as they performed as amateurs in the middle of the dancing throng. Following the Franco-Prussian War and its effective end of the Second Empire's parties, the cancan continued to be danced socially and semiprofessionally in dance halls by the young seamstresses and laundresses of Montmartre who reputedly made every day a Mardi Gras with their performances. The cancan, as they performed it, was called the *chahut.* It was a physically demanding dance with five major steps: the high kick, the quick spinning of the lower half of one leg, the spinning of the whole body while holding one leg up near the head, the cartwheel, and a concluding flying split (which was usually combined with the kicking off of a male dancing partner's top hat). The dance halls where the *chahut*

CARMENCITA.

MISS KATE VAUGHAN

W. & D. DOWNEY
PHOTOGRAPHERS

COPYRIGHT

LONDON & NEWCASTLE
TO THE QUEEN

*top left: **Carmencita*** INTRODUCED A NOVEL VARIATION ON THE SKIRT DANCE TO AMERICAN AUDIENCES IN 1889: THE SPANISH DANCE. THE SPANISH DANCE WAS TECHNICALLY A FANDANGO AND WON CARMENCITA MANY ADMIRERS AMONG SOCIETY WOMEN SINCE IT WAS CONSIDERABLY MORE CHASTE THAN THE FRENCH CANCAN AND BRITISH SKIRT DANCE. AS WAS OFTEN THE CASE IN VAUDEVILLE, HER SUCCESSFUL ACT HAD MANY IMITATORS. THE MOST SCANDALOUS OF THEM WAS CAROLINE OTERO WHO USED HER STAGE CELEBRITY TO FURTHER HER MORE LUCRATIVE CAREER AS A PROSTITUTE AND MADE THE SPANISH DANCE A LITTLE LESS RESPECTABLE IN THE PROCESS.

*top right: **Kate Vaughan*** WAS CREDITED WITH THE INVENTION OF THE SKIRT DANCE IN 1873. IN 1876, SHE JOINED THE GAIETY THEATRE IN LONDON, THE CHORUS OF WHICH IMPORTED THE DANCE TO THE UNITED STATES IN 1888. ALTHOUGH VAUGHAN HAD MANY, INCREASINGLY BAWDY IMITATORS, SHE REMAINED AN ICON ABOVE REPROACH IN THE WORLD OF THEATRICAL DANCE.

opposite: THE SKIRT DANCE IN ITS MOST SUBDUED FORM.

right: THOUGH IT BECAME AN ALL-GIRL CHORUS-LINE DANCE, MEN ALSO DANCED THE CANCAN IN ITS NASCENT STAGE IN PARIS, AND WERE SOMETIMES AMONG THE PROFESSIONAL PERFORMERS WHEN THE DANCE BECAME A STAGE ACT.

far right: DANCER **Ruby Winstone** DEMONSTRATES THE ATHLETI-CISM AND SHEER EXUBERANCE OF THE CANCAN. UNFORTUNATELY, THE DYNAMIC NATURE OF THE DANCE CANNOT BE CAPTURED IN A STILL PHOTOGRAPH. THE AGGRESSIVE, CEASELESS MOTION OF THE DANCE WAS WHAT MADE IT SO IMPRESSIVE TO AUDIENCES. THE POSSIBILITY THAT THE PERFORMER MIGHT NOT BE WEARING UNDERWEAR WAS ALSO CERTAINLY PART OF ITS APPEAL.

was performed were policed by an Inspector of Dance, a situation necessitated by the fact that few of the most popular dancers wore underwear under their bloomers. Since bloomers of the period were not seamed together at the center, the signature high kicks, cartwheels, and flying splits of the can-can were of exceptional interest to male observers. The Inspector of Dance at the Moulin Rouge addressed the situation by keeping a supply of safety pins handy to be provided to dancers who neglected to sew up their bloomers themselves. It was their version of the dance that became a profes-sional stage performance when Charles Zidler, in a flash of inspiration comparable to the invention of the wet t-shirt contest, decided to pay a group of dancers to perform nightly at his Moulin Rouge dance hall. The Moulin Rouge dancers toured England and America in the 1890s and adapted elements of Vaughan's skirt dance (mainly the skirt swishing) to their dance. The cancan as social dance and as a theatrical dance was adapted to American stages under various exoticizing titles (such as *quadrille realiste*), but was ultimately cate-

gorized under the catchall title of skirt dance. By the 1890s, cross-pollination between the British, French, and American skirt dancers resulted in many variations on the skirt dance, all of which were increasingly relying on the tease of flashing undergarments for their appeal even as they played to family-friendly American vaudeville stages.

There were also homegrown acts in vaudeville, which similarly belied vaudeville's claim of purity. One was a skirt dance of American invention: the serpentine dance of Loie Fuller. The serpentine dance was wholly distinct from the skirt, Spanish, and cancan dances. It did not have specific steps that could be imitated, but rather was based on the use of a voluminous white skirt that was made transparent by stage lighting. In the initial version of the dance, Fuller moved her skirt with her hands and spun around as strong stage lights, aimed from the front and back of her, alternately illuminated her swirling skirts or her body. The appeal of that transparent skirt (and whatever female body hap-pened to be underneath) caused Fuller's skirt dance to be widely imitated on the vaudeville circuit.

By 1900, skirt dancing was a full-fledged pop-culture phenomenon. Even a kiddie act such as *the Goldsmith Sisters*, pictured here, could do a skirt dance. Most of the dance's bawdy aspects had disappeared as it was made a part of the American vaudeville theater mainstream.

The Goldsmith Sisters

The cancan went from amateur performance to expression of athletic prowess to gratuitous flash of underwear inside of fifty years in its journey from Parisian dancing gardens to American Broadway stage. Ultimately, dancing skill took a back seat to the more reliable appeal of a pair of lacy bloomers.

LOIE FULLER'S SERPENTINE DANCE SWEPT VAUDEVILLE IN THE 1890S AS ANOTHER VERSION OF THE SKIRT DANCE. AT LEFT, *Minnie Renwood* WEARS AN IMITATION OF AN EARLY FULLER COSTUME. AT RIGHT, *Adelaide Early* WEARS A COSTUME BASED ON FULLER'S LATER WORK. BOTH PERFORMERS HELPED TO SPREAD THE DANCE, WHICH WOULD ECLIPSE THE TRADITIONAL HIGH-KICKING SKIRT DANCE IN THE NINETEENTH CENTURY.

THAT COME HITHER STARE. LIKE
STRIPTEASERS, SKIRT DANCERS HAD
TO MAKE A CONNECTION WITH THE
AUDIENCE—THEIR PERSONALITIES
WERE AS MUCH A PART OF THE ACT
AS THEIR DANCE ROUTINE. THIS WAS
ESPECIALLY TRUE IN HONKY-TONKS
AND BEER HALLS WHERE PERFORMERS
WERE OFTEN EXPECTED TO MINGLE
WITH PATRONS.

SCHLOSS
N.Y.

NOT JUST ANOTHER PRETTY FACE, *Eva Tanguay* WAS ONE OF VAUDEVILLE'S TOP DRAWS IN THE EARLY 1900S. AT THE CORE OF HER ACT WERE BAWDY SONGS, CHEEKY LANGUAGE, AND COSTUMES FEATURING TIGHTS TYPICALLY WORN BY BURLESQUE PERFORMERS. SHE ALSO MAINTAINED A BUILD THAT GAVE THE IMPRESSION SHE COULD HOLD HER OWN IN A BARROOM BRAWL.

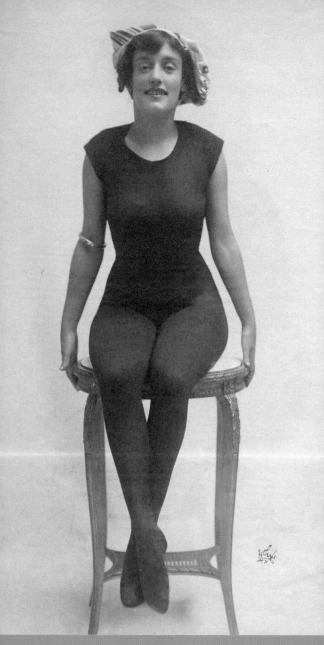

WHILE BURLESQUE FLESHINGS WERE BANNED FROM VAUDEVILLE
STAGES, *Annette Kellerman's* FLESHINGS-LIKE SWIMSUIT
WAS WELCOME. THAT THE THIN FABRIC WAS WRAPPED AROUND
A WELL-TONED BODY RATHER THAN THAT OF A VOLUPTUOUS
BURLESQUE QUEEN PROBABLY HELPED. ALSO, FROM THE LOOK
OF THIS PROOF FROM AN EARLY PHOTO SESSION (ABOVE LEFT),
KELLERMAN CERTAINLY DID NOT CARRY HERSELF LIKE A SEX
ICON EVEN THOUGH SHE WAS CONSIDERED ONE BY MEN IN THE
AUDIENCE. SHE ULTIMATELY PARLAYED HER DIVING AND SWIM-
MING ACT INTO A LONG CAREER IN VAUDEVILLE AND FILMS.

Another of the vaudeville sensations, wholly distinct from the skirt dancers, was Annette Kellerman, an Australian swimming champion who found fame pioneering the role of the bathing beauty with her diving act. Kellerman was an attraction at public beaches and amusement parks as well as on appropriately equipped vaudeville stages, and later in the movies. For her performances, she wore a one-piece swimsuit that, while covering her from ankles to upper arms, was much briefer than the average burlesque costume. Kellerman was arrested for wearing the suit on a Boston beach in 1907 and, although the charges were dismissed, interested members of the vaudeville audience were no doubt alerted by the press to the pleasures to be had from Kellerman's diving demonstration. Kellerman originated what would become a vaudeville staple, the tank act, as well as the sex symbol staple, the swimsuit model.

The lewd woman in tights also found her way into vaudeville in the person of Eva Tanguay, a top-paid performer on the vaudeville circuit in the early 1900s. Her success was built on her scandalous songs, such as "It's All Been Done Before—But Not The Way I Do It" and "Go As Far As You Like." Her bawdy lyrics and her performances in her signature pair of white tights were based directly on burlesque precedents. Tanguay's show was a throwback to Lydia Thompson's burlesque as she combined suggestive humor with a sex appeal based more on provocation than physical beauty.

Ultimately, vaudeville was not so much a clean entertainment as much as it was a popular entertainment. The strategy of marketing shows as good, clean fun was highly effective and middle-class audiences came, stayed, and were generally not overly shocked at the same show of legs that made burlesque the renegade entertainment

during the same period. Once the successful circuit could offer impressive salaries, legitimate stage actors such as Sarah Bernhardt did tours and drew an even wider audience to vaudeville. And though it was never completely respectable, vaudeville functioned, like burlesque, as a farm league for a growing entertainment industry in America. The stars of vaudeville would go on to populate Broadway revues, films, and then television as the vaudeville circuits died out.

The success of the women of the burlesque circuit and the various dancers who graced the stages of variety and vaudeville houses laid the foundations for the invention of striptease. The woman in breeches, cancaneuses, and bathing beauties proved the drawing power of the sexually provocative woman in all forms of popular entertainment, even in the supposedly repressive nineteenth century. The evolution of American show business gave women who had previously been hustling drinks for saloon owners or acting as the leisure time activity of wealthy men, the opportunity to step up on the stage and make a vocation of their sex appeal. Although only burlesque will admit paternity, striptease has roots in all of the nineteenth-century popular theatrical forms. By the 1950s, it was the last act from the populist theater of the turn of the century still drawing an audience. The only real difference between the nineteenth- and twentieth-century woman on the stage was the amount she had to strip in order to tease. ✩

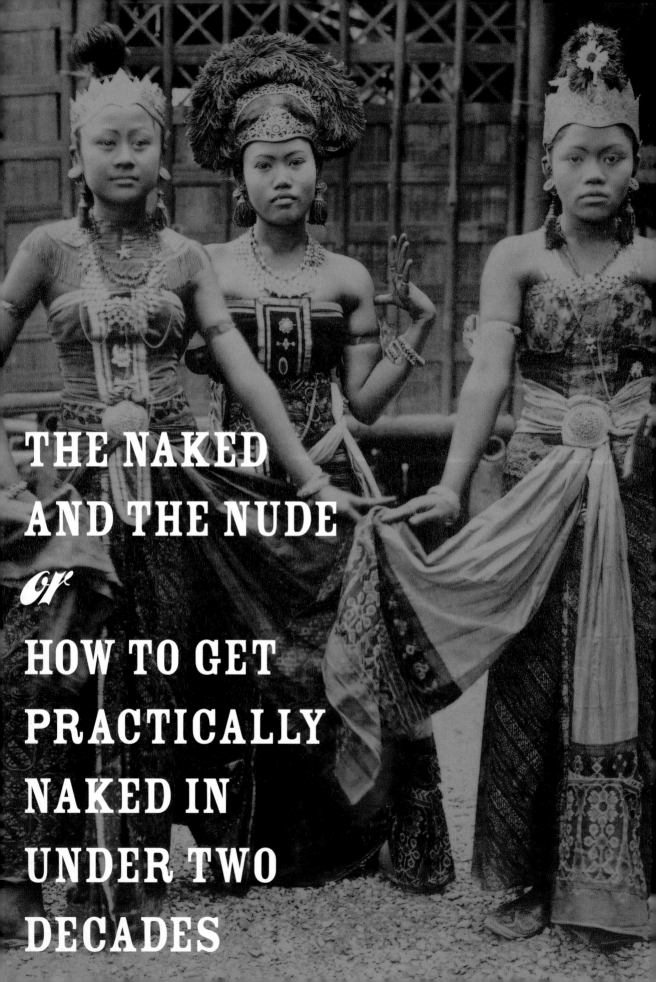

THE NAKED AND THE NUDE

or

HOW TO GET PRACTICALLY NAKED IN UNDER TWO DECADES

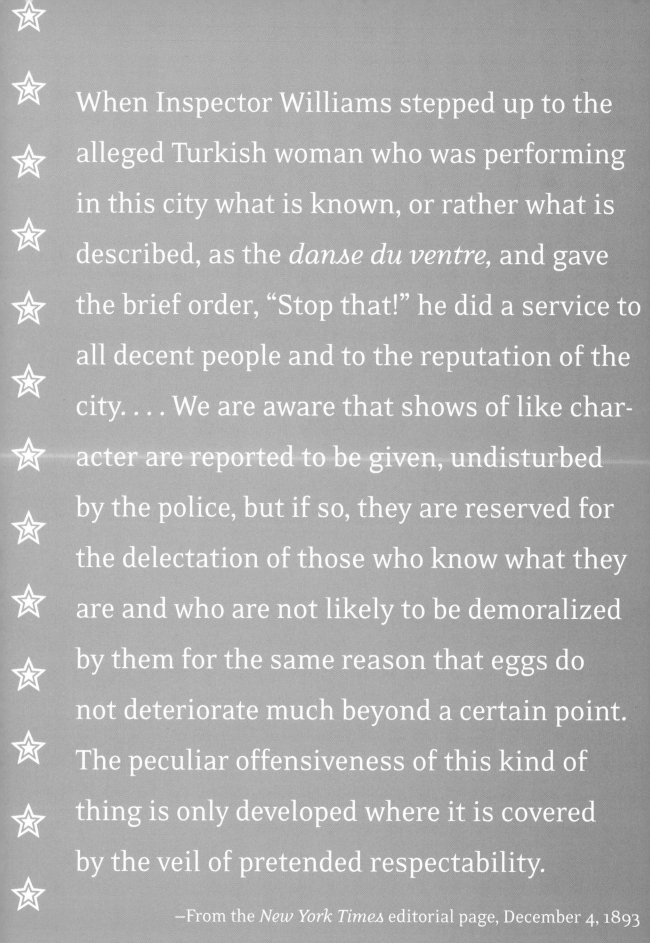

When Inspector Williams stepped up to the alleged Turkish woman who was performing in this city what is known, or rather what is described, as the *danse du ventre,* and gave the brief order, "Stop that!" he did a service to all decent people and to the reputation of the city. . . . We are aware that shows of like character are reported to be given, undisturbed by the police, but if so, they are reserved for the delectation of those who know what they are and who are not likely to be demoralized by them for the same reason that eggs do not deteriorate much beyond a certain point. The peculiar offensiveness of this kind of thing is only developed where it is covered by the veil of pretended respectability.

–From the *New York Times* editorial page, December 4, 1893

DESPITE THE SCANDALIZED TONE OF THE AFORE-QUOTED editorialist, the fact is that even as late as 1893, the exhibition of shameless women on the stage in America was pretty tame. Nudity or nakedness was rare, if not impossible. Though the term "practically naked" was often applied to female performers in the late nineteenth century, any significant amount of exposed skin was a rarity. This would change irrevocably in the decades that followed as performers such as Little Egypt, Loie Fuller, Isadora Duncan, Ruth St. Denis, and Maud Allan changed the standards for, and meaning of, the presentation of a woman's body on stage. Before them, the only Victorian ladies giving men a peek of flesh were confectionery ideals confined to the galleries and salons of Victorian artists. And there, the naked was called the nude.

The fine art nude was comfortably ensconced in Victorian society as a result of its undeniably illustrious history in Western art, dating back to the classical era. Nudes, classical to contemporary, were in the process of being categorized, analyzed, and catalogued in newly established museums by men who had recently invented the profession of art historian for themselves. These cultural arbiters considered the marble or oil-painted nude an expression of the human soul, not an affront to decency. They made this distinction via a standard of context: a painted naked woman was a nude if she was presented in the context of a grand or ideal thought. If the woman was a Greek nymph, a Roman goddess, an odalisque, or perhaps the personification of the dawn at sportive play with an anatomically incorrect satyr, she was nude. This led to a plethora of paintings of nubile, somnolent, and impossibly pink women reclining in clouds or on waves whose pulchritudinous presence in the artist's salon or wealthy man's home was justified by titles such as

Twilight or *Venus.* However, if the painted lady was not enveloped in ethereal mists and instead was depicted in the mundane confines of the parlor— and if she too closely resembled a less than idealized version of the Victorian man's wife or any one of the number of poverty-stricken prostitutes whom Victorian men of means plowed their way through—she was naked, not nude, and therefore not an appropriate subject for fine art. Meanwhile, the fact that the women who posed as models for the high art nudes generally were drawn from the ranks of Victorian prostitutes served to keep matters confusing.

This vague standard was bound to be abused. Such was the case with London Academy artist Robert Kemm's painting *The Slave Mart at Stamboul* (1890) which was critically panned by Americans for ostensibly being a morally uplifting painting about the evils of the slave trade, while it seemed clearly intended to display women of different ethnic backgrounds in various states of undress. Such mediocre art fueled objections to the nude despite general support from the academies of England and France and from middle-class mouthpieces such as the *New York Times.* When objections were voiced, however, the defense was swift and coldly condescending, as in this 1892 response to would-be defenders of public morals by the Hanging Committee of the Pennsylvania Academy of Design, which was published in the *New York Times:*

> You assert that certain pictures admitted by us
> to this exhibition are flagrantly indelicate. You
> speak of them as ruthlessly assailing your modesty, and say that their presence has been a direct
> attack upon the delicacy of your daughters and
> the morality of your sons. Heaven forbid that the

A PAINTING OF A BARE-BREASTED BEAUTY IS THE CENTER-
PIECE OF THIS WELL-APPOINTED 1908 PARLOR.

Annette Kellerman EVOKES *The Birth of Venus* IN A STILL FROM
THE 1916 FILM *A Daughter of the Gods*.

delicacy and morality of children should be so
poorly established as to be in danger of overthrow
by the contemplation of such pictures as you
have selected for censure. . . . [W]e cannot refrain
from expressing our sincere pity for that man or
woman who finds in all the beauty and purity of
the human form nothing but immodesty, indeli-
cacy, and, alas, indecency.

The importance of this defense is that it could just
as easily be applied to any naked body on display
and, in fact, it was.

The first naked performer of the Victorian
stage was the "nude" of the tableau vivant. Tableaux
vivants, also known as "living pictures," "living
statues," "posing acts," and "plastic poses," were
flesh and blood imitations of well-known art works.
Although they did not necessarily feature nudes,
the ones that did were the only legal way to display
a nude woman on the stage. Although tableaux

vivants have primarily been associated with stage
nudity, that is not their complete history. They
originated in France with the purpose suggested
in the translation of the term—to create a living
picture. In the beginning years of the nineteenth
century, tableaux vivants were a strictly upper
class amusement. In France, the tradition of private
performance of tableaux vivants was given a royal
seal of approval during the reign of Napoleon III.
At his autumn vacation château of Compiégne,
effectively the grand hotel of his regime, guests
passed the time by participating in tableaux
depicting *The Dream of Herculaneum* and the more
risqué *Sardanapalus on the Pyre with the Women
of His Household,* among other diversions. This
French tradition was imported to America as a part
of the celebration of Mardi Gras in New Orleans
where tableaux vivants were used as a spectacle
at private balls as early as 1857. These tableaux
served to entertain the idle rich both as an art

top: AN 1885 TABLEAU VIVANT, AS PRESENTED IN
THE FOURTEENTH STREET THEATER IN NEW YORK
CITY. THE POPULARITY OF TABLEAUX VIVANTS
EBBED AND FLOWED DURING THE LATTER HALF
OF THE NINETEENTH CENTURY. WHETHER IT WAS
INTENDED TO BE AROUSING REMAINS IN THE
EYE OF THE LONG-DEAD BEHOLDERS. IT DOES
REFLECT THE UNRETOUCHED REALITY OF FLESH-
INGS AS USED TO IMITATE A WORK OF ART.

left: THIS CIRCUS ENDEAVORED TO REVIVE GREEK
ART WITHOUT FORGETTING TO MENTION THE
"LOVELY LADIES" INVOLVED.

appreciation lesson and a form of titillation for
the more rakish set of wealthy men. It was the
latter form of tableaux vivants that was first
democratized and spread from the private homes
of the rich to the male-dominated spaces of
American concert saloons and then on to other
popular venues.

By the 1870s, the sanitization of American
variety shows into vaudeville entailed the excision
of "posing acts," although they would live on in
the men-only back rooms of dime museums, in
burlesque theaters, and at the far end of the carnival midway. Censors overlooked these decidedly
indecent tableaux because their defenders appro-
priated the defense of the high-art nude as valida-
tion of their existence. The popularity of the nude
in the mainstream of high art gave the rowdy
American concert saloon an effective defense
against obscenity laws, especially as the "artistic"
nude was being depicted in increasingly titillating
forms in the salons of London and Paris. The more
stimulating tableaux vivants were also protected
by the fact that the actual degree of nudity was
not quite as full as advertised. Some tableau
vivant models performed in shadow behind fabric
screens—they would appear in as convincing a
degree of undress as necessary and pose in imitation of some well-known nude, although they were
never actually naked. They were policed, nonetheless, by censors in case they might betray some
small movement. In the oversight of tableau vivant
performance, censors were preoccupied with movement. As long as performers remained static, they
remained within the law. Even into the early 1900s,
movement was only allowed between poses. Other
models performed on the open stage wearing
fleshings, and relied on their corsetless state to
render them nude. It was not until early in the

twentieth century that some tableau vivant models
performed topless and by that time there were
far more blatantly erotic breasts on display at the
Metropolitan Museum of Art.

By the 1890s, the popularity of tableaux vivants
was reaching its peak in more domestic contexts
in the United States. It was re-embraced as a parlor
entertainment with church groups, children, and
young unmarried adults arranging themselves into
"classical" groupings. A little over a decade after
the revival of privately performed tableaux vivants
in the United States, "posing acts," once banned,
were readmitted to the vaudeville stage.

While tableaux vivants represented one type of
nude performance at the turn of the century, that
of the undraped, unmoving figure, the Oriental
dancer typified another, more fearful type—that of
jiggling, uncorseted flesh. The rapid undulation
of belly, hips, and shoulders that characterized
the Oriental dance was in sharp contrast to the
established order of sexual display in the tableau
vivant. The very freedom of movement allowed in
Oriental dance was simultaneously titillating and
horrifying. It reflected a wholly different set of
values about the body from those reflected in the
discreet provocations of the tableau vivant and
the flash and tease of an ankle in the skirt dance.
To the Victorians, Oriental dance was, like all
things Oriental, exotic and desirable.

Oriental art and decorative objects of various
kinds had been of interest to Western nations since
Marco Polo established the first trade routes. The
particular variety of Orientalism that was in vogue
during the 1890s was the result of the commence-
ment of trade with Japan negotiated by Commodore
Matthew Perry in 1854. By the 1870s, the results of
the opening of that market were seen in the influence of Japanese design on artists such as James

THE ORIENTAL DANCER GOT HER INTRODUCTION TO AMERICAN AUDIENCES THROUGH THE IMAGINATION OF WESTERN PAINTERS OF THE ORIENTALIST SCHOOL IN PARIS AND THE UNITED STATES. ALTHOUGH ORIENTALISTS PRIDED THEMSELVES ON PRECISE ATTENTION TO ETHNOGRAPHIC DETAIL, THEY WERE WILLING TO EXPLOIT WESTERN FANTASIES OF ORIENTAL FEMALE SUBMISSION TO CREATE DRAMATIC PAINTINGS. *Jean-Léon Gérôme's* The Dance of the Almeh IS SUITED TO THAT END. IN HIS 1863 PAINTING, HE DEPICTS AN ALMEH, ONE OF A CLASS OF MIDDLE-EASTERN WOMEN WHO WERE DANCERS AND OCCASIONAL PROSTITUTES DURING THE NINETEENTH CENTURY. ALMEHS WERE ALSO PRACTITIONERS OF THE SO-CALLED "BELLY DANCE." PAINTINGS SUCH AS THIS ONE CREATED A DESIRE FOR THE EXOTIC ORIENTAL WOMAN THAT WAS LATER EXPLOITED BY CLEVER PROMOTERS ON THE MIDWAY OF SEVERAL WORLD'S FAIRS.

McNeill Whistler and Edouard Manet, as well as on art and decorative objects dealers, such as founder and promoter of the Art Nouveau movement Samuel Bing. The more popular explosion of all things supposedly Japanese was reflected by the wildly successful Gilbert and Sullivan play *The Mikado,* first performed in the United States in 1885 and revived several times in the years immediately following. By the 1890s, the fad was not limited to Japanese culture and the Orient had become a theme at the ballet, the opera house, and in both legitimate and burlesque theaters. Americans seemed willing to purchase anything advertised as Oriental–home decor magazines

exhorted readers to purchase decorative fans, parasols, and wall hangings at novelty stores that had premiered in the United States in the 1870s and which were widespread by the 1890s. And if genuine objects could not be had, European and American manufacturers would kindly provide facsimiles. For the dedicated (and decidedly more upscale) follower of all things Asian, there were also scenes of Middle Eastern and Eastern life provided by a group of French painters and some American followers known as, naturally, Orientalists. These paintings depicted scenes from Oriental life in painstaking detail–showing equal effort applied to the intricate designs on the tiles

MOLLY MACK.
ALLEN & GINTER'S
VIRGINIA BRIGHTS
CIGARETTES,
RICHMOND, VA

MISS PRAEGER
ADMIRAL CIGARETTES

ORIENTALISM WAS SWIFTLY ABSORBED INTO BURLESQUE
COSTUME, FIRST IN THE FORM OF "ARTISTIC" ACCENTS
SUCH AS THE FANS AND KIMONO USED BY *Molly Mack*,
AND LATER AS GENERALIZED EXOTIC COSTUMES OF
INDETERMINATE ORIGINS.

of the baths as to the lustrous bare flesh of the barbarously underclad Oriental women.

The interest in the Orient was piqued at the International Expositions of the nineteenth century that provided advertising for Oriental objects of all kinds, including the female kind. It was in this context that the Oriental dance was introduced to Victorian audiences. It was presented not as a legitimate cultural production on par with the European ballet, but as an object of anthropological study and oversight—another of the White Man's burdens (albeit a most appealing one). The first female Oriental dancers to make an impression on American culture and stage were the Javanese dancers of the Paris Exposition of 1889. They made such an impression on Exposition audiences that one year after their performances, the American premiere of the play *Cleopatra* starring Sarah Bernhardt featured "the strange Nubian style of dancing, which came into vogue at the time of the recent exposition." While it remains difficult to establish what the "strange Nubian style of dancing" was, it is dubious that the dancers in *Cleopatra* were imitating it accurately. But never mind the dance. The play likely featured costumes in imitation of the Javanese dancers seen at the Paris Exposition and those costumes alone, heavily bejeweled and exposing bare shoulders and, even worse, bare midriffs, would have sufficiently stimulated the audience's "bald heads" (common period slang for dirty old men). Though the "Nubian" erformance in *Cleopatra* was considered somewhat vulgar, it was not overtly attacked by the critics because of the unimpeachable status of any production featuring Sarah Bernhardt.

Such was *not* the case with the infamous performance of the dancer Little Egypt at the International Exposition and World's Fair in Chicago in 1893. Little Egypt's identity remains in question to this day, but her performance of a belly dance at the Fair's "Street of Cairo" has secured her fame, no doubt in part due to the hue and cry raised against her and her dance. In an open letter to the Fair's organizers, the Secretary Masters of the National Association of Dancing Masters called for an end to the "objectionable national dances by Algerian women and natives of several Oriental countries." Despite the lack of specific charges against the dances or dancers, Fair organizers censured the Persian Theatre at the Fair, and put the Algerian Theatre and the "Street of Cairo" under surveillance within days of the letter. This was despite (or possibly because of) the fact that the midway on which the dances were performed was the most well-attended section of the World's Fair, and that the "Street of Cairo" turned out to be the most popular venue at the Fair.

There were actually four different dancers performing at the "Street of Cairo" theater, and it is unclear who, if any, was the real Little Egypt. They all performed solo dances dressed in "a short bolero with coin decorations, a white chemise, harem pantaloons and a wide sash." The dance was most likely based on the *Kathak*, technically an Egyptian non-belly dance that was incorrectly identified as a belly dance by the Fair's midway manager, Sol Bloom. The *Kathak* consisted of movement into various graceful poses using a scarf as part of the choreography. Ostensibly, the performance also contained elements of the true belly dance, or *Raks Sharki,* which was characterized by undulations of the body and stamping feet. An amalgamation of the two dances was the one that ultimately spread across the United States.

By the end of 1893, the exotic Oriental dancer was beginning to replace the skirt dancer as the

THIS UNASSUMING LITTLE GIRL
WAS ONE OF THE *Egyptian*
dancers WHO CAUSED A FUROR
AT THE 1893 WORLD'S FAIR.

most shocking and titillating form of entertainment in America, and censorship was instituted accordingly. An example of this is the case of a group of Oriental dancers who performed in New York City. They were advertised as the same dancers from the 1893 Chicago World's Fair although it is not certain that they were. The story follows a pattern that would become typical of the harassment of exotic and striptease dancers in the twentieth century: Four women took the stage one at a time at the Grand Central Palace on Lexington Avenue and 43rd Street as part of a "World's Fair prize winners" show. In the audience, among "elderly men," "some well-known frequenters of the Tenderloin district," and "[a] number of ladies . . . evidently from very respectable families," was one Inspector Williams. Though the women's costumes were "modesty itself compared with the average ballet girl's costume," Williams ended the performance by approaching one "writhing" dancer and instructing her to "Stop that!" Although the performance that night never resumed, manager Adolph Delacroix defended the dancers saying their dance was "far less immodest than the ordinary skirt dance." The following day, the dancers performed again, were arrested, and were brought before a judge. The judge concluded that the dance could go on until a final decision was made. The dancers' lawyer defended them saying their dance had "been given before the crowned heads of Europe." The dancers performed for two more days and then had their day in court—which attracted a crowd of onlookers in the court's gallery and featured a "large and burly" policeman who "attempted an imitation" of the dance as did a Sergeant Archibald, much to the amusement of the gallery. The dancers were fined fifty dollars apiece and went back to work that night with a few changes

to their dance program that made it more resemble a typical skirt dancing performance.

The unanswered question in this and other accounts of early Oriental dance is, what was so wrong with the Oriental dance? One problem was that the Oriental dancer was a highly sexualized figure, not only in the high art of Orientalist painters and the popular art of variety halls, but also in the period's literary pornography, which was rich in lustful Turks, kidnapped European women, and beautiful, submissive harem dancers. Indeed, the four dancers from the Chicago World's Fair did not need to behave in a sexually provocative manner in order to be considered sexually provocative: they were sexually provocative types.

The other issue for the Victorian viewer was the absence of a corset in the Oriental costume. The corset was considered a necessity in the nineteenth century as a way to control the flesh, which the Victorians didn't like to see shaking or moving at all. To see it jiggling, wriggling, or convulsing in any way called into question a great many cherished assumptions Victorian men liked to maintain about the capacities and desires of their middle-class wives. So, although the absence of a corset was ethnographically correct for Oriental costume, it was still considered a form of nakedness by the Victorian observers. The consequence of its absence was the "writhing" judged so obscene by Inspector Williams and the equally irate *New York Times* reporter. It would seem, therefore, that the problem with Oriental dance was that it involved, for want of a better expression, shaking it. "It" being that thing. That thing which Victorian women generally encased in yards and yards of fabric. And there it was—jiggling, convulsing, and writhing. In public. In front of ladies. Next, they would probably all be doing it. Ultimately, Inspector

Williams was right to be concerned, but he would not be able to stop it. In its disposal of the corset, Oriental dance was one of the pioneering sources of the growing popularity of uncorseted fashions.

It is impossible to know whether the dancers who were arrested and fined in New York City were the same as the ones who performed at the Chicago Exposition, especially since the upshot of the Little Egypt scandal at the Chicago World's Fair was that "Little Egypt" became a franchise of sorts and remained one well into the twentieth century. After 1893, a "Street of Cairo" was erected at the midway of Coney Island. The "real" Little Egypt and other Oriental dancers became a mainstay at burlesque houses and carnivals across the United States. From this franchise came the term "exotic dancer," and suddenly fresh-faced factory workers' daughters from hole-in-the-wall towns in middle America could start a career in, say, Indo-Haitian interpretive dance, as long as they were willing and able to forgo their corsets, wear a few rhinestones on their tops, don loose pants, and writhe convincingly. These girls weren't striptease artists yet, but they paved the way for the birth of striptease by replacing the high-kicking chorus as the hallmark of burlesque with their own solo dances. The franchising of Little Egypt also changed the nature of burlesque performance by further separating the male comics from the female performers, making way for the female performers to finally go out on their own.

Although Little Egypt and those of her ilk would figure prominently in the direction taken by burlesque and striptease performers in the twentieth century, there is one performer without whom none of the performance pioneers of the 1900s would have been possible: Sarah Bernhardt. Bernhardt was the Victorian Barbra Streisand, the carte de visite Madonna. She was world famous and by all accounts lived a fabulous life involving many lovers, temper tantrums thrown with impunity, and the nightly adulation of thousands. She was an icon and the originator of a synergy among the sexually arousing modes of display possible on stage in her era. She portrayed herself at once as the artistic nude, the Oriental woman, and the performer of the tableau vivant during her career—all while remaining a practitioner of high art. As the commentaries on her performance in the 1890 play *Cleopatra* reveal, Bernhardt was able to inhabit both a sexually provocative and unassailably reputable space in the public imagination simultaneously. One reviewer notes of her costume for her performance that "every motion undresses [Bernhardt] almost completely," but immediately amends that assessment to say, "I mean, of course, in outline, for the long robes are perfectly straight, plain, and chaste." The question of Bernhardt's "undress" is later discussed in the fashion pages of the *New York Times*:

It may be rather late to go into much detail concerning Bernhardt's dresses as Cleopatra, but I could not refrain from joining in the infectious merriment of the actress when I related to her the growing legend of the six meters of crepe required—the only covering for her graceful, supple figure. "Mon Dieu!" cried Sarah, "I should be *nue* in a *quart d'heure.*"

And easily she might; for, although the studied poses are quiet and tranquil in their change, yet Sarah is constantly moving, and her robes, cut in what one may faithfully call the princess peplum outline, are quite firmly sewed. . . . Sarah's arms and neck are quite *au point* now, but she has absolutely no hips and no *ventre* so that these

Sarah Bernhardt WAS THE QUEEN OF
THE NINETEENTH-CENTURY PARISIAN
STAGE, BUT IT WAS HER WILLINGNESS
TO SLUM IT ON THE AMERICAN VAUDE-
VILLE CIRCUIT THAT MADE HER AN
IDOL TO THE LIKES OF LOIE FULLER,
ISADORA DUNCAN, AND MAUD ALLAN.

Loie Fuller GAINED HER FAME AS A SKIRT DANCER, BUT HER LASTING
CELEBRITY WAS A RESULT OF HER INNOVATIONS IN STAGE LIGHTING
AND COSTUMES. THESE INNOVATIONS CHANGED THE AUDIENCE'S
EXPERIENCE OF HER PERFORMANCE AND, AS A RESULT, SHE WAS ABLE
TO BECOME AN "ARTIST" AND SHED THE POPULIST TAINT OF THE
LABEL VAUDEVILLE SKIRT DANCER.

clinging robes remain chaste, while they outline the figure in each pose. How more developed Cleopatras are going to manage I should rather imagine than see.

Thus, concerns about Bernhardt's indecency are laid to rest while the suggestion of her nudity is alluded to again. She is at once naked and clothed, much like a tableau vivant performer behind the safety of a screen. The controversy over Bernhardt's costumes makes the concern over the various Little Egypts more comprehensible as their performance was based on the movement of their flesh—not just the sight of it. Bernhardt's costume controversy also reveals just how easily the standards of decency were transgressed in 1890. The vague and delicate nature of Victorian propriety would be an effective publicity tool for performers who would follow in Bernhardt's footsteps. Successful heirs to Bernhardt's fame and status would follow her example of high art performance, while borrowing heavily from the sensational nature of Little Egypt.

Although the women who would set the tone for sexually provocative performance for decades to come all faced some censure for their work, they would in fact mimic the career trajectory already established by Bernhardt. Loie Fuller was Bernhardt's earliest heir and also her contemporary. In Bernhardt's tradition, she styled herself as an artist, playing with the boundaries of the audience's acceptance of the high art nude. Fuller had her New York stage debut in 1886 in a central boy's role—common casting for an ingenue at that time. In 1889 she became stranded in London following the failure of a play she had produced and starred in, and found a job at London's skirt dancing mecca the Gaiety Theatre. Following her sojourn at the Gaiety, Fuller began perfecting her solo per-

ALTHOUGH REFERRED TO AS A SKIRT DANCER EARLY IN HER CAREER, *Isadora Duncan* REFUSED TO ACCEPT THAT TITLE. IN THIS 1899 CABINET CARD, SHE REINFORCED HER REFUSAL BY REJECTING THE PETTICOATS OF THE SKIRT DANCER IN FAVOR OF A COSTUME MADE FROM HER MOTHER'S LACE CURTAINS.

formance, which consisted of her dancing dressed in a voluminous skirt made of thin fabric rendered transparent by back lighting. Although her contemporaries called Fuller's performance a skirt dance, it was not "skirt dancing" as dance historians would later define it—it lacked the acrobatic high kicks and flying splits that were characteristic of the form. Dubbed the "serpentine dance" by the theater owner who, in 1891, put Fuller into his variety show *Uncle Celestin,* the dance evoked the less reputable form of the tableau vivant wherein a naked woman was displayed behind a fabric screen. Fuller *was* dressed, but only in a thin, white silk fabric. As that fabric was illuminated,

"Show us your tights!" Even out-side of the burlesque circuit, the "boy's" role, played by young ingénues and requiring tights, was a rite of passage for young female performers in the American theater. These costumes provided the audience with the nineteenth-century equivalent of gratuitous nudity. *Loie Fuller*, pictured here, participated in this tradition before she found fame with her serpentine dance.

Ruth St. Denis's EXOTIC DANCES "RADHA" (LEFT) AND "EGYPTA" (RIGHT)
SET A NEW BAR FOR THE AMOUNT OF NUDITY ALLOWED ON THE VAUDEVILLE
STAGE WITHOUT SETTING OFF ANY ALARMS. SHE WAS ABLE TO BYPASS
THE SCRUTINY OF CENSORS THROUGH THE SUPPORT OF SOCIETY WOMEN
WHO CONSIDERED HER PERFORMANCES LEGITIMATE EXPLORATION OF
EASTERN CULTURES. THE PERFORMANCES WERE THAT, BUT THEY WERE
ALSO AN EXPLOITATION OF WESTERN PERCEPTIONS OF THOSE CULTURES
AS SEXUALIZED AND DECADENT.

her body was revealed. Fuller's act relied mostly on the mere suggestion of her nudity, but even that suggestion was enough to excite and titillate audiences.

The serpentine dance was the high point of *Uncle Celestin* and it was widely imitated. In response to her imitators, Fuller continued to develop new dances using light and fabric to sculpt new forms on the stage. In all of the acts she performed, titillation remained an important element. Fuller was able to get away with this by positioning her dance as "art"—she danced as the personification of the serpent, the butterfly, and the clouds, familiar themes to the Victorians who were accustomed to seeing the same imagery in paintings and sculpture. By 1893 she had established herself as a hit in Paris on the stage of the Folies-Bergère and, in a reversal of the tableau vivant, artists flocked to paint and sculpt Fuller in performance.

Fuller's transition from skirt dancer to respected solo dancer and artist's muse was the result of what might be called visionary chutzpah—a quality she held in common with many dance artists who followed her. The dance that brought her initial fame (and which was disseminated across America by imitators in vaudeville and burlesque) was the result of an aging ingenue's search for a good gimmick. Fuller was not a trained dancer and by all accounts the serpentine dance wasn't much of a dance. Its success relied on the revelation of Fuller's legs and on the innovative lighting techniques she used to effect that. As Fuller's career progressed during her Paris sojourn at the Folies-Bergère, she continued to develop her costume and lighting effects. She started using long, hand-held wands to direct the motion of her ephemeral silk dress. Along with this, she designed a set that consisted of a glass platform that illuminated her body from

below giving her dances a slow motion, dreamlike effect. Fuller became and remained wildly famous in Europe and the United States over the next twenty years. In 1900, she even had her own pavilion at the Paris Exposition and was sculpted by Auguste Rodin. She had elevated the skirt dance to epic stage spectacle and became the first female performer to effectively evoke and surpass the luminous nudes of the salon paintings who floated in clouds and waves.

Fuller's performances created a new, ambiguously defined space on the stage for the solo dancer as an artist. She called into question the strict separation between "clean" vaudeville and "dirty" burlesque on the American stage as she was showing off less than the average burlesque star of that period, but suggesting more. While the music halls of London and Paris allowed for a certain amount of latitude between the decent and indecent in performances, American stages were strictly separated into family-friendly vaudeville theaters and bawdy burlesque houses. While the separation was never as strict as vaudeville promoters would have their audience believe, it allowed for less freedom of expression than European venues. Fuller's ephemerally suggestive style marked the beginning of the end of vaudeville's narrow rules for female performers. Fuller further contributed to the development of the new style of dance performance by directly assisting up-and-coming performers, including ones who would further destabilize the separation between clean and dirty with their increasingly direct presentation of the nude on stage.

Isadora Duncan, who was briefly one of the beneficiaries of Fuller's support, was able to further transgress Victorian strictures of what a woman could reveal on stage. The daughter of a bohemian California family, Duncan started her career as a

Eva Tanguay's SALOME.

right: EVEN TWENTY YEARS AFTER
HER DAYS AS A SKIRT DANCER, *Ruth
St. Denis* STILL RECOGNIZED THE
DRAMA OF SWIRLING FABRIC AND
MADE IT A PART OF THE COSTUMING
FOR HER EXOTIC DANCES.

bottom: Isadora Duncan's STATED
INTENT OF REVIVING GREEK ART IN
DANCE SOUNDED LIKE THE FAUX-
INTELLECTUAL HYPE OF A DIME
MUSEUM "PROFESSOR," BUT HER
SUCCESS WAS UNDENIABLE. THE
REALISM OF HER EVOCATIONS OF
GREEK NYMPHS AND THE FRIEZES
OF ANCIENT ARCHITECTURE PUT
SOLEMN, WHITE-FACED CIRCUS
TABLEAUX VIVANTS TO SHAME.

teacher of social dance and then became a chorus girl in 1895. In 1899, she debuted a solo dance performance interpreting *The Rubaiyat of Omar Khayyam* at a matinee performance for a group of wealthy society women who had become her patrons. Several of the women walked out on her debut, not because they were unwilling to accept her unorthodox choreography, but because in her short, thin chemise, she was perceived to be about as naked as it was possible to get and still wear clothes. And in truth, even through modern eyes, the skimpy, cotton tunic Duncan wore seems flimsy. Duncan added to that provocation by regularly dancing, rather than just posing, imitations of Greek art. Duncan, unlike the stocking-clad women performing in both legitimate and indecent tableaux vivants, moved freely about the stage in between her poses—skipping, turning, and smiling. In the context of traditional imitations of the classical, it was shocking. Duncan's dancing went far beyond the slight movement that was only recently allowed between poses in tableaux vivants. Natural movement—the basis of Duncan's choreography—being performed on a public stage by a woman wearing so little clothing was a clear affront to Victorian propriety.

Still, Duncan got away with it. And not only that, she got away with it while gaining prestige and respect as an artist. Duncan had the advantage of having chosen dance in the "Greek tradition" as her form of exotic dance. As Bernhardt and Fuller before her, Duncan gained acceptance for her dance by positioning it as art. Once labeled an art form, her dance became elevated in the eyes of her patrons while still giving her an opportunity to reveal a great deal of skin, as Duncan interpreted "Greek tradition" to mean requiring only a thin chemise over bare legs and feet. However sincere

Duncan may have been in her stated desire to rediscover Greek dance, it is impossible that she was unaware of the consternation her perceived undress would cause.

The acceptance of her dance was also based, in part, on the audience's level of comfort with the tableau vivant, both as a stage entertainment and as a parlor game. Further, the audience was familiar with the idea of moving through a series of poses, as was done in the theatrical acting of the period and in pantomime. Duncan's performances combined the upper-class, popular, and lascivious interests in tableaux vivants and transformed them into the building blocks of modern dance alongside that other acknowledged influence on avant-garde dance, the dance of the "exotic."

Duncan managed to pull off an impressive feat for someone who was essentially putting a new twist on the exotic dancer tradition of showbiz hype. Her innovation was to apply a veneer of intellectualism to her performance. As her career progressed and she found her way to London through letters of introduction from her New York society connections, Duncan danced accompanied by lecturers on Greek culture. By 1904, the year of Duncan's first success on the Paris stage, she had begun to follow her performances with her own lectures on her philosophy of dance. Duncan's pretensions obscured the probability that she was as much a huckster as any carny to ever extol the virtues of a harem beauty. She claimed she had no formal dance training, when in fact she had studied with skirt dancer Katti Lanner during her chorus girl years. She also gave multiple, conflicting accounts of her background to reporters over the years. Still, Duncan's pretensions and her initial performing career as a society women's pet performing at high tea protected her from the carnival taint that lowered the status of other exotic dancers. A 1908 reviewer noted, "In Miss Duncan's dancing there is the spirit and poetry of things suggested. There is no hint of the personality of the artist. Neither is there tone of sensuous or sensual. The dancer's costumes appear merely a background for her art." Duncan went on to dance for years after and founded several schools of dance. At the end of her life in 1927, that she had accepted an invitation to found a dance school in the Soviet Union proved more scandalous to Americans than her relative state of undress at the turn of the century.

Following a path similar to Duncan's was her contemporary and fellow modern dance pioneer, Ruth St. Denis. St. Denis started as a skirt dancer in 1894 at a typical dime museum in New York City called Worth's Family Museum and Theatre. She performed six shows a day alongside attractions such as an albino musician, the human billiard ball, a trick dog, and a pickled calf. Within a year, St. Denis moved into chorus and small speaking roles that she continued performing for the next ten years. In 1904, she was inspired by an ad for Egyptian Deities cigarettes to create an Egyptian exotic dance. The result was the dance theatrical *Radha* which was equal parts sideshow, serious research, and mass-market Orientalist imagery. St. Denis was probably more of an intellectual than Duncan, but she allied herself more closely to exotic dance of Little Egypt. She even admitted to getting ideas for her dances on the carnival midway at Coney Island. Her claim for the credibility of her dances was based on her assertion that she had gone on to learn the *real* Oriental dances and therefore was not a cheap carny, but a serious scholar of Eastern dance. This claim was both true and misleading. St. Denis did in fact research the "true" dance of India (as opposed to merely imitating carnival belly dance). Her research was shallow at first, but became

increasingly serious as her dance career continued. However, as much interest as St. Denis had in presenting "true" Oriental dance, she had more in finding an act that would allow her to break out of the tertiary roles of a chorus dancer and into the big time as a celebrated solo dancer and serious artist.

New York hostess and tastemaker Mame Fish who initiated society patronage for St. Denis embraced the dance St. Denis introduced. By 1906, St. Denis was able to put on a showcase of her dance for New York theater managers who were unsure what to do with the act as it was a bit too intellectual for a vaudeville stage, the appeal of St. Denis's apparent willingness to perform with a bare midriff notwithstanding. Ultimately, St. Denis's success would come from the patronage of society women and at the matinees that they attended, not from rowdy, populist vaudeville stages. At those matinees, St. Denis performed a combined Oriental and skirt dancing choreography of turns, waltz steps, and undulations of arms and back, all concluding in poses that might suggest the imagery of Hindu deities or the Art Nouveau femme fatale. This amalgamation of forms is clearly reflective of the audience's indifference to distinctions among Asian cultures and Western portrayals of them. Also at those matinees St. Denis reduced her initial costume of beaded jacket, harem pants, and over-skirt to silk fleshings with jeweled chains to better evoke the Victorian vision of the Indian goddess. St. Denis not only rehabilitated Oriental dance for middle-class consumption, but she also established it as the second thread of modern dance with Duncan's dance style as the first. She would remain popular up until World War I and ultimately gain a more far-reaching influence as the founder of the Denishawn dance school that produced famed choreographer Martha Graham, among others.

top left: **Maud Allan** WAS A CLASS ACT, AS THIS FEATURE
PHOTOGRAPH IN THE UPSCALE ARTS AND PHOTOGRAPHY
MAGAZINE *The Burr McIntosh Monthly* ATTESTS. SHE
WAS ALSO WELL AWARE THAT SHE WAS EXPLOITING HER
SEXUALITY IN HER ACT. UNFORTUNATELY, SHE WOULD
HAVE LITTLE MORE TO OFFER OF INTEREST TO AUDIENCES.
ALLAN DIED IN OBSCURITY, REMEMBERED ONLY FOR HER
SEXUALLY PROVOCATIVE "DANCE OF THE SEVEN VEILS."

top right: CONTORTIONIST **La Sylphe's** SALOME.

left: **Ruth St. Denis** TAKES THE FLESHINGS OUT OF THE
TABLEAU VIVANT IN FAVOR OF BODY PAINT IN THIS 1927
PHOTOGRAPH.

In retrospect, St. Denis and Duncan are identified as artists in part because of their strategic positioning of their dancing as high art, and also because each started her own school and trained dancers in her respective style. However, on their first appearance, they were taken for mere skirt dancers . . . and rightly so. It was only through their skillful manipulation of the ambiguous space between the naked and the nude that they were able to gain respectability. During their heyday, many other female performers presented "speciality" and exotic dances, to varying degrees of success. Among them, and considered an equal to or even superior to Duncan and St. Denis for a time was Maud Allan. She combined the high art, popular, and subtly pornographic elements of the tableau vivant being used by Duncan with the vaudeville version of Oriental dance being presented by St. Denis, into a wildly popular "Dance of the Seven Veils," entitled "The Vision of Salome."

Allan, like Duncan, was a daughter of San Francisco. She initially planned to be a concert pianist and went to Germany in 1895 to study music. Not long after her arrival, her brother murdered two young women at the family church and Allan was consequently advised by her mother to remain in Germany and drop the family name of Durrant. Allan did as she was advised and managed to avoid an overt taint of scandal while she lived in Europe. In 1903, having since abandoned her music studies and taken up dance, Allan had her stage debut in Vienna. In 1906, she premiered her Salome dance in front of a private audience of moneyed supporters of artistic dance. They were impressed with the piece, which led to other private performances including one for the Prince and Princess of Wales. With the royal seal of approval, the height of her success and fame came in London two years later.

THE DIAPHANOUS SKIRTS OF *Maud Allan's* SALOME COSTUME HAD A PRECEDENT IN THE BRITISH BURLESQUE COSTUME SHOWN HERE.

Her success started a craze for "Salome" dancing that spread throughout American vaudeville and burlesque venues, and included imitators with already established careers such as mimic Gertrude Hoffman who performed a "life-like impersonation" of Allan at Hammerstein's Theatre's roof garden in the summer of 1908, the contortionist La Sylphe, vaudeville star Eva Tanguay, and skirt dancer Blanche Deyo.

The popularity of Allan's dance was in great part due to her choice of subject matter. The Salome story is a gruesome and titillating melodrama sanctioned by its biblical origins. In it, Salome is both the step-daughter of King Herod and the object of his lust. His desire for her leads him to offer her anything she wants if she will dance for him. She complies and then demands the head of St. John the Baptist on a platter. Innumerable artists had painted Salome in various and increasing degrees of undress and her popularity as artist's subject justified the titillating brevity of Allan's (and others') Salome costume. The association of Salome to stripping, implied by various artists' renditions, was implied more explicitly by Oscar Wilde's play *Salome* in which she was described performing the "Dance of the Seven Veils." The paintings and Wilde's play all heavily influenced Allan's dance and, although she didn't strip off her veils, she did deliver an all but unobstructed view of her legs, midriff, and arms. Only her lower torso and her breasts were fully covered. Allan did wear a skirt, but its fabric was so sheer it appeared completely transparent, even more so than the back lit serpentine skirt worn by Fuller or the fine chemise worn by Duncan.

Ruth St. Denis described Allan's dance as "an adaptation of Isadora Duncan's Greek Spring [dance], the costumes and actions of some of the German actresses in the part of Salome, and a generous sprinkling of my arm movements during all of her numbers." Of course, Allan's arm movements could not have been directly taken from St. Denis's since each of their dances had premiered simultaneously on different continents. Although St. Denis's slightly hostile account must be read in the context of having been compared unfavorably to Allan in the London press, she correctly suggests that Allan's dance combined natural movement from pose to pose, pantomime, and Oriental dance moves. It had all the advances of modern dance wrapped around story that featured virginal lust and the gore of a severed head. The dance could hardly fail.

By 1910, Allan's dance, as widely imitated in the United States, had some versions reputedly delivering on the promise of nudity. According to vaudeville historian Joe Laurie Jr., it was Eva Tanguay who finally "discarded all seven veils." In truth, Laurie's account seems dubious since Tanguay's fame in 1910 was such that if she *had* stripped completely, there would be many contemporary accounts of it, and there were none. Still, as Salome dancing and its attendant idea of seven veils to be removed were absorbed into the American theatrical imagination, stage nudity became possible. The combination of dancing, posing, Oriental imagery, and barely veiled nudity that had made a success of Maud Allan and her followers was taken up by Broadway producers and transformed into ostentatious revue shows. Once the nudity of the tableau vivant and the shimmy of the Oriental dance had made it on to the Great White Way, they were reabsorbed into the more prurient entertainments, and the name "striptease" was coined to describe the resulting performance. And by then the nude on stage had a mainstream imprimatur that would make its censorship nearly impossible—and a real live naked lady wasn't such a rarity anymore. ⭐

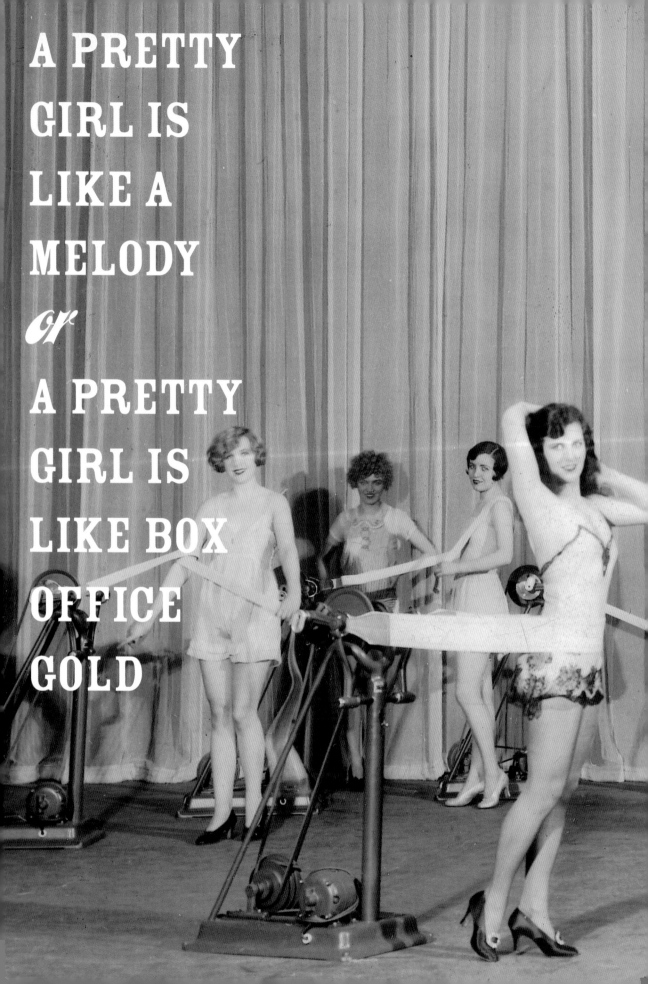

A PRETTY GIRL IS LIKE A MELODY

or

A PRETTY GIRL IS LIKE BOX OFFICE GOLD

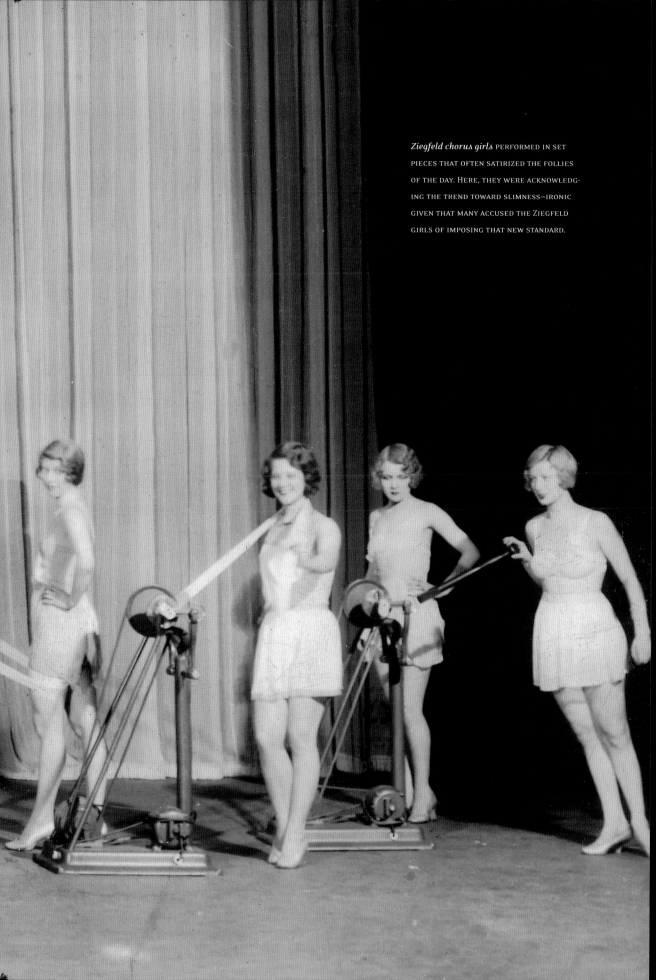

Ziegfeld chorus girls PERFORMED IN SET
PIECES THAT OFTEN SATIRIZED THE FOLLIES
OF THE DAY. HERE, THEY WERE ACKNOWLEDG-
ING THE TREND TOWARD SLIMNESS—IRONIC
GIVEN THAT MANY ACCUSED THE ZIEGFELD
GIRLS OF IMPOSING THAT NEW STANDARD.

Many dancers on the stage today are vulgar because they conceal and do not reveal. They would be much less suggestive if they were nude. Yet they are allowed to perform, because they satisfy the Puritan instinct for concealed lust. That is the disease that infects Boston Puritans. They want to satisfy their baseness without admitting it. They are afraid of the truth. A naked body repels them. A suggestively clothed body delights them. They are afraid to call their moral infirmity by its right name.

—Isadora Duncan on women on the stage, 1922

AFTER THE 1908 INTRODUCTION OF SALOME DANCING, THE artistic nude of vaudeville was poised to be transformed into a lucrative show business commodity. This would be accomplished by the establishment of a new theatrical form on the Broadway stage, one in which the prototype dances established by Isadora Duncan, Ruth St. Denis, and Maud Allan could be copied and repeated to form the anonymous line of show girls whose bland perfection and opulent costuming signified the high life of the 1920s. These girls, like the original modern dancers in beauty but unimpeded by pretensions toward any particular thought or theory of their purpose on the stage, were the building block of the American revue that overtook Broadway from about 1907 through the late 1920s.

The invention of the American revue is generally credited to Florenz Ziegfeld Jr. who staged the first of many *Ziegfeld Follies* in 1907. This explanation, of course, is too simple to actually be true. The American revue was an amalgam of French, British, and American popular theatrical forms reinvented under Ziegfeld's brand name—it was really only new to uptown Broadway theaters. The initial concept, suggested to Ziegfeld by his then common-law wife Anna Held, was simply to restage the Parisian Folies-Bergère show for New York audiences. It worked spectacularly well as evidenced by the $120,000 profit made by the first *Follies*.

American vaudeville producers had been raiding European theaters for talent going back to the nineteenth century. In England, variety acts had been featured at music halls in urban centers that had become popular around the beginning of the nineteenth century. Originally created as a venue for bar patrons to put on skits and sing popular songs (while presumably getting righteously wasted on strong drink), music hall performance

became increasingly professionalized over the course of the nineteenth century. In 1868, John Hollingshead founded the Gaiety Theatre in London. The Gaiety featured the same kind of popular songs and skits that had characterized the music halls, but placed more emphasis on the girls in his chorus—selected based on beauty first and talent second. It was the Gaiety chorus on which Ziegfeld hoped to model his own.

An equivalent development of popular theater was happening in France in the nineteenth century. The Paris neighborhood of Montmartre had become an entertainment center even before the nineteenth century due to its location outside the gates of Paris where wine was taxed at a lower rate. The lower prices led to the establishment of thriving bars and an attendant group of entertainers. These venues, known as cafe chantants (or concert cafes), were similar to American concert saloons, featuring alcohol, coffee, and performers who worked for throw money. By the 1880s, the cafe chantants were a part of Europe's music hall circuit and the Folies-Bergère was at the top of the heap as the best known and most popular. By the turn of the century, European music halls had developed into easy pickings for American producers looking for variety acts with a Continental flair. It was there that Ziegfeld found his first Broadway star.

The music halls of London and Paris were a long way from the world of young Florenz Edward Ziegfeld Jr. Born in Chicago on March 21, 1867, the son of a pianist and music conservatory director, Ziegfeld was probably intended by his family for more prosaic, if respectable, things than the popular theater. He showed early signs of rebellion in his fascination with the American Wild West (one he shared with many young men of his generation). In his mid-teens, he briefly sought work with the

The London Gaiety Girls, WHO WERE REASONABLY MODEST AND TENDED TO MARRY WELL, WERE A PROTOTYPE FOR ZIEGFELD'S CHORUS.

opposite: The Folies-Bergère WAS THE TOP VARIETY STAGE IN PARIS, HOSTING LOIE FULLER AND ANNA HELD, AMONG MANY OTHERS. IT WAS FROM THE FOLIES THAT FLORENZ ZIEGFELD JR. CLAIMED TO HAVE DRAWN MUCH OF HIS FORMULA FOR THE ZIEGFELD *Follies*.

Buffalo Bill Wild West Show—the 1880s equivalent of running away with the circus—but didn't stay long. Instead, he spent ages eighteen through twenty-six working for his father's music college, which serviced the upper crust of Chicago society and provided a good living for the entire Ziegfeld clan. In 1893, Ziegfeld's father was elected to the board of commissioners for the International Congress of Musicians at the 1893 World's Fair. The commissioners conceived an ambitious slate of programming for the Fair, but only the more populist offerings of music and children's choruses drew audiences. Ziegfeld must have learned from his father's experience because that same year he branched out from the high-culture confines of the conservatory and became the manager of a vaudeville house.

The theater Ziegfeld managed, The Trocadero, presented a vaudeville bill that was fairly typical for the day: a strong man, a cornetist, a singer of popular songs, and a Spanish dancer. But the involvement of someone of Ziegfeld's social and cultural status with vaudeville was far from typical. Ziegfeld was undaunted, however, and made a hit of his opening night with the attendance of Mrs. Potter Palmer, the leader of Chicago society and a woman who was generally not seen at vaudeville theaters. While manager of The Trocadero, Ziegfeld signed strong man Eugene Sandow to a management contract. It was at this point that he truly launched himself as a theatrical impresario and master marketer. Ziegfeld promoted Sandow not only by conceiving inventive demonstrations of his strength, such as inviting audience members to sit on a platform that Sandow would then lift, but also by promoting Sandow as a sex symbol. Ziegfeld would invite women audience members to come backstage after shows and touch Sandow's muscles. This proved to be a successful promotion as high society women were apparently susceptible to the lure of the flesh.

Knowing a good thing when he found it, Ziegfeld took Sandow to vaudeville houses in New York City and San Francisco, and then assembled a full bill of vaudeville acts, including Sandow, and toured the nation through 1895. Unfortunately, Ziegfeld gambled away most of the money he earned from that tour. Now broke, he approached comedian Charles Evans and convinced him that he could produce a revival of Evans's successful comedy *A Parlor Match*. Evans was sold on the idea and Ziegfeld went to Europe to find a star for the play. It was in Europe that Ziegfeld found his inspiration for the American revue in the form of skirt dancer Anna Held.

Anna Held claimed to have been born a Catholic Parisian in 1873. In fact, she was born to Jewish parents in Warsaw around 1870. Her family immigrated to France in 1881, and Held began her show business career there singing on the streets for loose change. After her father's death in 1884, Held and her mother moved to London and Held established herself as an actress in London's Jewish

ANNA HELD AND HER HUSBAND, FLORENZ ZIEGFELD, JR., INSPECTING THE LATEST PRODUCTIONS OF THE PARISIAN MODISTES, WITH A VIEW TO THE COMING WINTER'S THEATRICAL CAMPAIGN

1908

UNTIL THE ZIEGFELD *Follies* WERE FIRMLY ESTABLISHED IN THE MID-1910S, *Florenz Ziegfeld Jr.* USUALLY GOT SECOND BILLING TO HIS COMMON-LAW WIFE, *Anna Held*, AS THIS CARTOON ILLUSTRATES.

theatrical community. In 1887 she returned to Paris and began to perform on the music hall circuit touring France, England, Holland, Germany, and Norway. At first, her act consisted of sad love songs, a very popular form in the cafe chantants, but in 1895 she began to perform more upbeat tunes punctuated by joyous and revealing high kicks. The new act was a hit as was her song "Le Colignon," which she performed dressed in a cab driver's uniform complete with skin-tight pants and a whip. By 1895, Held had already been mentioned in the American press by influential New York theater critic Alan Dale. In 1896, Ziegfeld discovered the already-established star and offered her the starring role in *A Parlor Match*.

Anna Held WAS THE PROTOTYPICAL
ZIEGFELD GIRL IN TERMS OF GLAM-
OUR, FAME, AND SEX APPEAL. HER
BODY TYPE, HOWEVER, COULD NOT
HAVE BEEN MORE DIFFERENT FROM
THAT OF THE ZIEGFELD BEAUTY.
HELD WAS REPRESENTATIVE OF THE
LATE-NINETEENTH-CENTURY FEMI-
NINE IDEAL: SMALL, WASP-WAISTED,
AND TOP HEAVY. AFTER 1908, THE
CORSET AND BOSOMS FELL OUT OF
FASHION AND HELD AND ALL HER
LESSER IMITATIONS IN VAUDEVILLE
AND BURLESQUE WERE RENDERED
OBSOLETE AS TALL AND SLIM
BECAME THE NEW IDEAL.

left: ZIEGFELD KEPT HIS GIRLS
IN THE PUBLIC EYE WITH
CONSTANT PUBLICITY STUNTS,
SUCH AS ANNOUNCING THAT
THE GIRLS WERE GOING TO THE
BEACH TO HAVE A SWIMMING
CONTEST.

below: ZIEGFELD OFFERED A
GIRL FOR EVERY TASTE.

Held accepted the role and returned to New York with Ziegfeld. The choice was a good one. Their match would be a commercial and romantic success and by 1897, following a successful run of *A Parlor Match,* the two were living together. Held and Ziegfeld continued to work together for the next fifteen years and, in a way, she was the original Ziegfeld girl, except that she was as much her own invention as she was Ziegfeld's. Their greatest success together was 1906's *The Parisian Model,* which revealed Ziegfeld and Held's risqué approach to early-twentieth-century theater. Among others, the play featured a scene in which Held changed costumes behind a "screen" of chorus girls, and a scene in which the chorus girls laid on their backs on the floor and "kicked-out" a song with the jingle bells that had been strapped to their ankles. This was not Ziegfeld's first foray into early intimations of the striptease. In his 1898 production, *The Turtle,* one scene featured an actress removing her bodice, skirt, and corset and then retreating behind a glass screen to complete her undress— yet another version of the tableau vivant. Held's European origins and her considerable talent gave cachet to her risqué performances, elevating them above similar stage numbers in burlesque. Ziegfeld gained prominence through his association with Held, allowing him to create a stage iconography that would rule striptease performance into the 1950s, while vehemently denying ever being involved with striptease at all.

Ziegfeld's collaboration with the very French Held prepared him to "invent" the American revue. His emphasis on its European origins obscured the very American sources of the revue. A French spelling of the word "revue" and an invocation of the Folies-Bergère made it plausible for American audiences to ignore the fact that, to a great degree,

Ziegfeld's *Follies* was essentially a variety show imported uptown to the Great White Way. Ultimately, Europe's only real contribution to the American revue was an exotic accent on the marketing pitch and the lack of strict separation between the "clean" and "dirty" entertainment it offered.

The first revue Ziegfeld put together, at Anna Held's suggestion and with her chorus as the top-billed attraction, would set the trend in popular entertainment for the next two decades by both drawing the skirt dancers and modern dancers into the Broadway mainstream and by, eventually, redefining them as the products of an impresario's skilled image making. That definition, however, would be the result of years of retrospective myth making on Ziegfeld's part. In 1907, at the premier of the first of twenty-four *Follies,* the press rightly recognized the revue as "a vast vaudeville show" and Ziegfeld was mainly recognized as "Anna Held's husband."

Although the *Follies* would become the defining entertainment of the 1920s, it started out as part of a recognized trend for upscale vaudeville, as vaudeville venues remodeled their theaters and their entertainments after the Wintergarden in Berlin and the Folies-Bergère in Paris. *The Follies of 1907* was essentially a series of musical acts slightly organized around a satire of the ridiculous aspects of contemporary culture. Its looseness was intentional and the press playfully noted that librettist Harry B. Smith was threatened "for damages if by any mistake a plot should be unearthed."

Ziegfeld's *Follies of 1907* premiered in the summer season in the Rooftop Garden of the New York Theatre. Roof gardens were another innovation of upscale vaudeville. Conceived in imitation of European beer gardens and cabaret restaurants, they offered a performance space for the summer months when most New York City theaters were

Fanny Brice CAME TO THE
ZIEGFELD *Follies* FROM THE
BURLESQUE HOUSES OF THE
LOWER EAST SIDE. SHE WASN'T
PRETTY ENOUGH, OR "ALL-
AMERICAN" ENOUGH, TO BE A
ZIEGFELD GIRL, BUT SHE WAS
AN ACCOMPLISHED COMEDI-
ENNE. SOME OF HER BEST BITS
WERE SATIRICAL TAKES ON THE
BURLESQUE WOMEN WHO WERE
POINTEDLY EXCLUDED FROM
THE *Follies*.

NOT ALL ZIEGFELD GIRLS WERE
TALL AND THIN. A LITTLE MEAT
WAS ALLOWED IF IT CAME WITH
SOME TALENT FOR DANCING OR
SINGING. THEY WERE MOSTLY
RATHER YOUNG, THOUGH—SOME
ZIEGFELD CHORINES WERE AS
YOUNG AS FOURTEEN.

uninhabitable due to the heat. Ziegfeld's *Follies* were at first indistinguishable from most of the other roof garden shows. It was planned as a satire of the events of the year and was structured much like a variety show would be: a big opening number with a full chorus and showgirls, a tableau vivant, a comic scene or song, a spectacle, a song, a comic sketch, a song and dance number, a comic sketch, a dance, a specialty act, and a full company finale, and then a second act with more of the same. The defining factor that separated the show from variety was money. Ziegfeld put a great deal of money into production and costume design (and put more and more into them as the *Follies* continued to be produced). He also spent a lot of money buying the best talent out of other shows, including many of the star comedians of the burlesque houses such as Fanny Brice, Eddie Cantor, Leon Errol, and Bert Lahr. One thing Ziegfeld didn't steal from the burlesque houses was the girls. Although Ziegfeld placed the girls at the center of his productions, as did the burlesque houses, he avoided using the same types of girls, that is, lower class, immigrant women who dominated the variety and burlesque stages. Ziegfeld wanted to sell the titillation of the burlesque stages, but with his own, personal imprint. His only real contribution: the Ziegfeld girl—beautiful, reasonably talented, very well groomed, decidedly nonethnic, and available for the price of a theater seat.

When Ziegfeld staged his second *Follies* in 1908, its principal appeal was identified by critics in what would become a constant refrain of show reviews:

> It is a colorful entertainment, and the color has
> generally been laid on with good taste, several of
> the ensemble dances being more than ordinarily

beautiful, and a series of song pictures reproduc-
ing the work of a popular illustrator, who draws
beautifully fluffy young ladies, being artistic as
well as pretty.

Pretty girls in living pictures, having been sancti-fied by the work of Isadora Duncan, were now ready for mass consumption. Ziegfeld would go on to create a veritable factory for the production of pretty girls artistically displayed. And under his direction, the naked or the nude (depending on the viewer's perspective—literally and morally) would make it onto the Broadway stage to the thunderous applause of masses of theatergoers.

The very first *Follies* of 1907-1911 were "cyclonic vaudeville of an elaborate order," with an emphasis on the girls. *The Follies of 1907* featured Salome dancer Mlle. Dazie. The touring company of *Follies of 1908* featured contortionist and Salome dancer La Sylphe. By 1909, Ziegfeld had contracted the always-provocative Eva Tanguay for the show, not incidentally on the heels of her arrest for violating blue laws on costuming for a Sunday concert she had given in a vaudeville theater. Ziegfeld also featured showgirl (and his mistress) Lillian Lorraine in a bathtub ostensibly wearing only soap bubbles. The Ziegfeld emphasis on girls must have been profitable because by *Follies of 1911* "the show was mostly girls and glitter."

"Glorifying the American Girl" became Ziegfeld's motto for the *Follies*. He discovered girls, he finished them, and then he turned them out onto the *Follies* stage, presumably to party hard, marry well, and live happily ever after. Ziegfeld became a sort of Fairy Godmother. For the duration of the *Follies*, as many women were buying the Cinderella story as men were looking for an eyeful of glorified girl. Ziegfeld had perfected the process of glorification while

top left: One of the secrets to the success of Ziegfeld's shows was that he spared no expense where costumes were concerned. This led to beautiful shows and kept the full attention of the women in his audience who liked to imagine themselves at the center of all that lavish care.

top right: An example of the innovative costuming that made Ziegfeld first among equals as a revue producer. The costume was designed not for the *Follies*, but for Ziegfeld's *Midnight Frolic*, a dinner dance with a stage show that was offered after the Broadway shows let out for the night. This nightclub-style entertainment was very popular in the years before prohibition. Due to the high spirits brought on by the spirits served, this particular costume rarely survived the night intact. Wayward, or possibly well-aimed, cigarettes would pop the balloons over the course of the evening. This gimmick was one stripteasers would later elaborate, creating costumes made entirely of balloons.

right: Ziegfeld, the man, the brilliantly promoted and wholly self-created myth.

FLORENZ ZIEGFELD

left: The tasteful Ziegfeld nude. In this picture, the viewer can see nothing except that the showgirl is naked under the lace shawl. Most of the Ziegfeld showgirls had portraits such as this one taken.

bottom: In keeping with the well-established tradition of the tableau vivant, Ziegfeld presented his first nude as a scene from the ride of Lady Godiva. A morality tale and a true story to boot, no one could possibly call it obscene.

working with Anna Held: he paid newspaper men to write stories about her; he had posters of her put up in store windows; he had her picture published in *Police Gazette*; he arranged for a theater critic to "surprise" her in her negligee; and he planted a story in the newspapers that she took daily milk baths. As he applied this process to choruses of *Follies* girls, he simply credited himself as the creator of both the girl and the fantasy surrounding her.

And there was another side to this fantasy that appealed to the men in the audience—that perhaps they could hope to have their pick of the chorus. The plausibility of this fantasy was increased by rumors that Ziegfeld had already played Prince Charming as well as Fairy Godmother to a number of his star showgirls. The sexual availability of the Ziegfeld girl was central to her appeal as behind-the-scenes accounts of revues clearly illustrate in their salivation over "a chorus rehearsal . . . [where] the privileged visitor will find anywhere from twenty to sixty girls, in costumes obviously designed to permit free movement of anything the director requires freely moved." It seems logical that identification with that director was a short, simple step for men in the revue audience. Ziegfeld had again taken a page from the late era (and more disreputable) burlesque shows' marketing ploys where the chorus girls were equated by polite society with promiscuity. If a chorus girl was being pursued by a stage door Johnny, he made sure it made the paper. If one got drunk and danced on a tabletop, he arranged for a photographer to capture it all. As he became a celebrity, publicizing his own affairs took care of itself. By all of the orchestrated accounts, being a Ziegfeld girl wasn't just a job, it was a lifestyle.

The early *Follies* were part of the mainstream, but they were also a bit cheeky. Taking place in New York City theater roof gardens, they were more akin to an intimate cabaret than the stage spectacle they would later become. The cabaret business Ziegfeld helped found became well entrenched in New York City as a means of fleecing tourists. The old lobster palaces of the late nineteenth century where robber barons went to cheat on their wives with courtesan/skirt dancers such as La Belle Otero were increasingly converted into cabarets or nightclubs following on the heels of Ziegfeld's success. They redecorated and advertised themselves as the real, naughty New York experience catering to visiting tradesmen and their wives. With its mass production in musical restaurants and nightclubs, the intimate variety entertainment Ziegfeld had been perfecting would become an ultimately joyless and mechanical experience, as pointed out by essayist Richard Barry in 1912:

> Never fear that you will miss this spirit of carnival. It is on tap nightly from 6 o'clock until 1 in the morning. There is no necessity for any one to miss it. It is there, ready for the picking at a dollar or a dollar and a half a pick, any evening you are in the humor. In fact, there is no chance to miss it. Consequently, there is no chance at all to achieve it.

As a matter of survival, Ziegfeld evolved and expanded the *Follies*.

He did so by spending more and more money on sets, costumes, and girls. He also pushed closer and closer to onstage nudity, which would ultimately call the attention of censors to all revues. As early as 1909, censorship had become a mild concern—an editorial in the *New York Times* noted, "There are exhibitions of dancing and nakedness in the limelight that would be out of place except in the criminal haunts of Paris and the private bathroom." Although the article seemed to call for action, the ensuing controversy soon devolved into a backbit-ing war of words among competing theatrical producers over whose performances needed to be censored (and thereby presumably removed from competition). Despite what New York's Archbishop called the "orgies of obscenity" going on the New York stage in 1909, the public seemed to like what they were seeing.

Ziegfeld's ambitions as a producer were rewarded in 1913 when his shows began to be reviewed in the theater column of newspapers, not alongside the vaudeville circuit. Still, he did not abandon lucrative cabaret-style entertainment completely. Rather, he diversified his productions, hosting the *Follies* on a proper stage while introducing the *Midnight Frolic* at the same theater's roof garden. Having established himself as an institution, there was nothing left to do but undress the Ziegfeld girl as prettily, expensively, and inventively as possible.

At the second *Midnight Frolic* of 1915, which featured women, as one reviewer put it, "pulchri-tudinous to a Ziegfeldian degree," Ziegfeld intro-duced costumes with balloons at the hem of the short skirts that could be popped by the cigarettes of the show's audience members. Another *Frolic* featured a raised runway with fans underneath which would turn on at random intervals as show-girls crossed it going to and from the main stage, revealing more than just a glimpse of stocking. Meanwhile, costumes at the *Follies* were shrinking noticeably: "[The] costumes are many and beautiful and occasionally aided by the low visibility which will account for some of the enormous patronage sure to favor the 'Follies of 1916'"; "The 'Follies' is . . . an exposition of the modiste's [dressmaker's] art, not to mention nature's"; "[A]t Mr. Ziegfeld's show we have some of the comeliest persons extant prancing about more or less clad in as lovely cos-tumes as the stage has ever known." *Follies* star Will Rogers noted that if the *Follies* did not glorify the American girl, it certainly exposed her. If the costumes shrank on dancing chorus girls, they seemed to disappear entirely from the Ben Ali Haggin tableaux that were *Follies* centerpieces. These spectacular living pictures were a prominent feature of Ziegfeld's early 1920s *Follies* and the pleasures they had to offer were circumspectly noted by theater critics: "[I]t is the eye that is mostly cajoled, particularly by an extraordinary set of what used to be called 'living pictures' arranged by the discerning Ben Ali Haggin."; "[I]n a Ben Ali Haggin picture, the unadorned feminine form came in for still further attention"; "The girls are there, gorgeously gowned as ever—wearing somewhat fewer clothes than usual this time in the Ben Ali Haggin tableau."; "[The girls] are carelessly but charmingly revealed in the familiar Ben Ali Haggin tableaux [sic]."

Just how much was revealed on Ziegfeld's stage remains somewhat of a question. It was cer-tainly more than ever before. Pictures of the era's chorus girls show the distance traveled from the burlesque leg show and the vaudeville skirt dance. Unencumbered by tights or fleshings, chorus girls were dressed in only a bikini's worth of material in some shows. And the women at the center of the tableaux were definitely topless, albeit with their hair carefully arranged. Delivering on the promise of nudity, Ziegfeld's glorified girl wasn't just a tease. And by 1920, Ziegfeld wasn't the only one glorifying girls.

Florenz Ziegfeld Jr. had many imitators on Broadway—he was making too much money *not* to have them. He also made it look easy. And maybe it was. His first major imitator (there were many minor ones) was George White, who premiered the

MODERN DANCER MEETS HAREM GIRL MEETS FEATHERED
SHOWGIRL. THE GLORIFIED GIRLS TOOK OVER VAUDEVILLE AND
BROADWAY REVUES IN THE 1920S. ZIEGFELD HAD CREATED
A GREAT GAUDY MONSTER OF FEMININE PULCHRITUDE.

left: The apex of Ziegfeld "glorification" became the basis for a showgirl uniform of feathers, rhinestones, and flesh-toned netting still being used by performers today.

---

right: Knowing a good ad campaign when they saw one, burlesque producers were among the first Ziegfeld imitators. One burlesque producer glorified *June Conrad* as the star of the 1916 burlesque show *Follies of Pleasure.* Ziegfeld sued to keep the term *Follies,* but would not be able to corner the market on expensively presented showgirls for long.

first of his *Scandals* series in 1919 to indifferent reviews but an impressive box office. White had come up as a vaudeville dancer who was one half of a two-man team working in small-time vaudeville houses. He discovered his ambition as a revue producer while spending a year as part of the *Follies* company. Within a year of producing his first revue, he found his legs in the genre with his well-received *Scandals of 1920.* White had identified Ziegfeld's formula fairly accurately and, following the time-worn showbiz tradition, proceeded to take it further: "[*Scandals of 1920*] was jazz, costumes, girls and bare legs—very many bare legs, despite the fact that they were sometimes covered with paint in lieu of other covering." In 1923 White had another hit with a variation on the living picture: a living curtain of "half a dozen undraped feminine forms" who apparently swung down from above at the end of the first act and remained dangling there as the lights blacked out. In 1924 the degree of nudity in one of White's touring companies proved too much for the Mayor of Chicago's Advisory Committee who reported that:

> A "doll chorus" required more clothing from the waistline up; that certain "living statues" should change their postures; that the "Sapphire Girl" should wear more sapphires; recommended the elimination of a part of a "looking glass" scene and decreed at least tights for certain living models.

Also in the field by 1923 was Earl Carroll who announced his presence on the revue scene and distinguished himself from other producers with a letter to the *New York Times* saying:

> My "Vanities of 1923" differs from all other revues—every bit of it was conceived in my own brain. I planned my structure and I lighted it, and I called in my trusted artists to carry out my conception. There was no helter-skelter rehearsing. . . . The spacious and beautiful Earl Carroll Theatre was ungrudgingly given up to these rehearsals, which I consider at least as important as the performances themselves. All the lyrics and the music were composed by me; [the] special blocks device used for speedy and effective changes throughout the revue was invented by me, and the various artists were engaged by me especially to suit the original conception I had in mind.

Carroll's productions were considered third string in comparison to Ziegfeld's and White's, but Carroll was more than Ziegfeld's equal in getting publicity. His first attention came from an appeal for chorus girls on a radio broadcast. The ensuing outcry by concerned mothers and the press caused the American Radio Association to call for legislation regulating broadcasting. Carroll took the opportunity to respond:

> There is no attempt on my part to lure any girls from their homes or firesides, as one writer put it. I am inviting these girls to meet me on the stage of my theatre as a purely business proposition.
>
> The usual procedure of inexperienced girls is to call at a theatrical agent's office, and he derives a fee if he is successful in obtaining an engagement for the girl. With my offer there is no middleman's profit. The girls pay no fee and they receive the greatest consideration.

Of course, given his well-cultivated reputation (one that was assumed of most other revue producers as well), consideration by Carroll might well involve a trip to the casting couch. The reading public knew

Earl Carroll's Vanities REVUES WERE THE LOGICAL CONCLUSION OF WHAT FLORENZ ZIEGFELD JR. HAD STARTED
IN 1908: GIRLS, GIRLS, AND MORE GIRLS. ONE OF CARROLL'S SHOWS FEATURED 108 GIRLS. *The Marmeins troupe*
(LEFT) AND *the Patterson Twins* (RIGHT) WERE A FEW AMONG MANY. WHILE CARROLL AND OTHER REVUE PRO-
DUCERS OFFERED MORE, THEY DIDN'T OFFER ANYTHING NEW OR BETTER. THE MARMEINS WERE YET ANOTHER
VARIATION ON THE SALOME THEME AND THE PATTERSON TWINS WERE JUST ANOTHER VAUDEVILLE DANCE ACT.
AND THE NOVELTY OF ALL THE ARTISTICALLY DISPLAYED FEMALE FLESH WAS WEARING THIN.

to take his protestations with a grain of salt. The tongue-in-cheek humor underlying his statement was reflective of the content of his revues, as was his public persona. Carroll's studied bombast extended to his stage shows, some featuring as many as 108 chorus girls. His chorus girls were not only the most numerous, but they were also reputedly the most naked, a reputation bolstered by Carroll's comical and probably well-orchestrated run-ins with censors and police.

Although by the 1920s Broadway revues were undeniably a part of mainstream American entertainment, the degree of nudity in them was not without some objection by professional moralists. The suggestion of censorship of revues and other farces and musical shows was first made by The New York Society for the Suppression of Vice, a group that was mainly a vehicle for the complaints of one John S. Sumner. In its report, the Society referred to the offending light theatrical fare as "orgies" (a word that does not mean what censors seem to think it means). The editorial page of the *New York Times,* while not in full concurrence, did suggest that some self-censorship was in order, if only to avoid the attention of the likes of Mr. Sumner. Nothing in particular came of The New York Society for the Suppression of Vice report until 1923, over two years after its publication, when a citizen's jury was planned to address indecency charges against plays. That citizen's jury was agreed upon by theatrical managers and the city's Commissioner of Licenses expressly on the grounds that it would not investigate the claims of the apparently very deeply concerned Mr. Sumner since "Action would [only] be taken on 'legitimate' complaints . . . meaning those of persons not professionally engaged in complaining." Four days following, the Police Commissioner announced that

he would investigate four plays at the request of Mr. Sumner. Soon, the crusade against obscenity (and, one hopes, orgies) was joined by the Society for the Prevention of Crime, Acting Mayor Murray Hulbert, and the Methodist Episcopal Board of Temperance, Prohibition, and Public Morals. "Sensual dancing and sensual costumes, or the lack of them" were the grounds for condemning shows of which Henry N. Pringle, Superintendent of the Society for the Prevention of Crime, had made "personal inspections."

Within a month of Sumner's complaint, a grand jury investigation was under way despite presiding Judge Cornelius F. Collins's disclosure "that the number of complaints to the police was not as large as might have been expected in view of recent comments from the pulpit and other sources." At the head of the inquiry was District Attorney Joab H. Banton, who took a hard line, stating:

> There is no reason why we should permit salacious
> plays to be presented in this city to please a lot
> of filthy-minded people from out of town. They are
> the ones that patronize such plays. The average
> New Yorker is clean-minded and is offended by
> these plays.

But the hullabaloo was over as quickly as it had begun. Literally days later, the District Attorney announced that "objectionable features" had been removed from the plays in question. He did not say what those features were. In fact, over the course of the reportage on the controversy, the title of the plays and the nature of their offense had never been disclosed out of fear of giving the plays undue publicity. The only real information contained in reports on the censorship battle was the names of the selfless politicians involved.

The battle would not stay quiet for long, however, and both politicians and revue producers would ably exploit it. In 1924, Earl Carroll refused to add "a fibre" to the costumes in his show after being ordered to do so by the Commissioner of Licenses, saying, "I deny that there is any offense to the law or to the public taste in nudity that is artistically presented." He later spent six well-publicized hours in jail over a painting of Vanities chorus girls by a Mr. Kessler displayed in the lobby of his theater. From his cell, he issued the statement that,

> Mr. Kessler's position as an artist is above reproach, and I would rather spend the rest of my life with this one lone cockroach and myself than be free to bump into a lot of long-haired, weak-chinned reform reprobates who see nothing but licentiousness in the living beauty of lovely girls.

And then he ordered dinner for himself and his cellmates to be delivered by taxi.

Opposition to stage nudity was heating up outside New York as well. In Baltimore, the hula-hula dancers in a play titled *Seduction* were ordered by police to increase their coverings, from the initial design of "some" veils, a belt, and trunks colored with flesh-tinted powder. In Philadelphia, the Superintendent of Police waited with a blanket in the wings of the theater hosting a touring company of the *Vanities* in case he should need to cover one of the performers. "The Superintendent was disappointed when the actress appeared in a costume that was far from startling." Even Ziegfeld did not escape censorship on the road. His *Follies* was canceled in Emporia, Kansas, due to vigorous protest against a previous revue in the theater in which his show was scheduled to appear.

In 1926, the police finally got a day in court with the revues. Beryl Halley, who played "Eve" in a scene in the revue *The Bunk of 1926,* was arrested for taking part in an indecent exhibition. The case was tried by Magistrate Harry A. Gordon who first asked to see Miss Halley's costume of a five-inch-wide fig leaf, a long blonde wig, a brassiere, and a dancing belt. He then said he would "learn for himself the extent of Miss Halley's costume," by attending the revue. After attending, "he went back stage, mounted four flights of stairs to Miss Halley's dressing room and in the corridor examined a blonde wig, a brassiere and a dancing belt handed to him by the actress, who was then wearing a kimono." Magistrate Gordon finally decided that:

> The fact that a gilded fig leaf is the chief adornment of a dancer does not necessarily mean that her performance is indecent . . . present day standards do not reasonably permit condemnation of a dancer who appears in scanty raiment in a scene not unlike what may be seen in paint, marble or bronze in nearly every art gallery.

But on the heels of the apparent legal vindication of the artistically presented showgirl, Ziegfeld himself, now the grizzled old guard of the revue scene, came out against stage nudity with the oft-used in-my-day argument against it:

> Under the artistic hand of Ben Ali Haggin I was the first to present his tableaux, a glorification of womanhood beautiful. These were intended as live paintings, bringing the master's brush to the human form in a gorgeous and resplendent setting. No immodesty was intended. It was meant for an extravagant and colorful display, and as such

This publicity photo from an ostensible "Queen of Burlesque" contest in Chicago shows the lessons that had been learned by burlesque producers in the Ziegfeld era. By 1929, even low-rent burlesque theaters were using publicity tactics invented and perfected by high-rent Broadway revues, although offering slightly less glorified girls.

By 1927, Ziegfeld announced that he would stop using the term revue "owing to the disrepute which [he] now believe[d] to be attached to that word."

District Attorney Banton took up the banner against revues again in 1927 following successful prosecution of Mae West's play *Sex,* but was apparently too late. The *New York Times* reported that:

> Nudity is at present on the decline, according to the reviewers. Most of the recent revues and musical shows have shown a reaction in this regard. The nude is said to have become passé on the stage, because of its over popularization by the night clubs.

By THE LATE 1920S, *Florenz Ziegfeld Jr.* WAS THE OLD GUARD ON BROADWAY. HE HAD HIS OWN THEATER AND HAD MOVED FROM PROMOTING HIMSELF AS THE GLORIFIER OF THE AMERICAN GIRL TO PROMOTING HIMSELF AS THE FOUNDER OF THE AMERICAN MUSICAL.

Still, Banton sent policemen to *Vanities* and *Scandals* only to find there was "no nudity on the New York stage at present of a character to warrant proceeding against the producers of musical shows," although the box office for both was up considerably due to his interest. But in October of the same year, Banton was still going on:

> I'm going to rid the New York stage of nudity. When necessary I'll back up patrol wagons to stage entrances and gather the performers in as they are, take them to the Night Court and show the Magistrate just what the audiences had to look at.

audiences reveled in the sheer beauty of the tableaux. Not having a Ben Ali Haggin to lead them, the bolder and more brazen producers, ready to ape any successful ingredient of a successful revenue, stepped out to present a rank imitation. The results, since there was no artistic mind to direct them, were sadly lamentable.

It is for this reason that I am leading the movement back to artistry and normalcy in the theatre. There is but one thing left for legitimate producers to do, and that is to lead not only audiences back to the shows based on merit and artistry, but to force other producers to amend their ways by a declining clientele surfeited with dirt and filth.

That response proved to be unnecessary. By 1929, the pendulum on censorship was swinging back as Actors' Equity Association began to lobby against censorship laws, pleading the case of actors who were being arrested for saying even one innocuous line in a supposedly indecent play. Instead of less, more and better nudity was on its way to the American stage. The striptease was about to arrive on Broadway. ☆

BURLESQUE
ON BROADWAY

or

THE RISE
AND FALL
OF THE
BROTHERS
MINSKY

Burlesque may or may not have upped the ante on nudity when it ascended to Broadway. It did, regardless, continue the tradition of justifying display of nudity through classical imagery. This rendition of Leda and the Swan was a feature at Billy Minsky's Republic Theatre. It was classical, but still a bit kinkier than what Ziegfeld might have offered.

The city feels that the exhibitors in burlesque houses for several years have been a disgrace to New York. They are cesspools of vice and indecency and are lewd and indecent to a degree almost unbelievable. I am submitting a police inspector's report, which is the filthiest thing ever presented in a court of record in this State or any other State.

If the people of the City of New York could read this evidence they would storm these theatres and tear them to the ground.

—ASSISTANT CORPORATION COUNSEL TO THE CITY OF NEW YORK,
Charles C. Weinstein, 1937

BY 1931, AS THE GREAT DEPRESSION SET IN, THE CONSPICU-
ously consumptive Broadway revues went into sharp
decline. Earl Carroll struggled to avoid bankruptcy
proceedings. Florenz Ziegfeld Jr. passed away and
his *Follies* went into dormancy. Meanwhile, burlesque shows, the dirty old uncles of vaudeville, were
booming. The form initiated by Lydia Thompson and
other women in tights had stubbornly persevered.

Just what was the big draw? H. M. Alexander
makes a firsthand account of the 1930s burlesque
show in his 1938 book *Strip Tease.* At a ticket
cost of $1.10, the show opens with a comedy skit
followed by specialty dancer Carmen Valencia.
Valencia parades across the stage wearing a white
dress as the live band plays. Toward the end of the
first song, Valencia drops the top of her dress to
flash her breasts and then winds herself into the
curtains as the lights black out. As the second song
begins, Ms. Valencia dances back out to center
stage with one arm covering her breasts and the
other securing her dress at the waist. Toward the
end of the second song, she reveals her breasts and
then unsnaps her skirt to reveal her left side from
ankle to ass cheek. Then she disposes of her dress
completely to be revealed in only a g-string. The
lights black out again and then come back on for
Valencia to take a bow from the security of the curtain. She finishes with a quick turn to flash her
ass to the audience. A production number and then
a comedy skit follow Valencia, and then stripper
Sylvie Sylvane takes the stage. Sylvane opens by
singing a bawdy song and then takes off her top.
She then does a grind (a move explained by
Alexander as writing the letter "o" with one's pelvis)
with her back to the audience and then turns and
does a series of bumps (pelvic thrusts) punctuated
by rim shots by the band's drummer. As the song
ends, she pulls off rip-away pants to show her

g-string. As an encore, she parades across the stage
and then pulls the curtain over her midsection and
removes her g-string and twirls it at the center of
the spotlight. And the crowd goes wild.

This, at last, was striptease. Alexander's report
on it reveals a number of moves that became stan-
dardized in the striptease of the decades that
followed: the "parade" entrance, the first flash of
nudity, the use of the curtain to prolong the tease,
the bump and grind, clothing gimmicks like conve-
niently placed snaps and rip-away pieces, and
the removal of the g-string to reveal . . . that the
g-string has been removed. These moves were the
synthesis of all the influences that had fed into
the striptease since the nineteenth century. The
parade went back to the earliest chorus girls, and
had been perfected by Ziegfeld's showgirls. The
flash and the protective curtain were elements of
the old tableaux vivants. The bumps and grinds
were the confluence of belly dance, modern dance,
and the jazz shimmy into one rhythm-punctuated
full-body writhe. And the clothing gimmicks were
pure vaudeville. This new admixture was the creation of the real popularizers of striptease, the star
dancers. But they would not have had a place to
perform had it not been for the steady creep of
burlesque onto Broadway.

As early as 1915, while Ziegfeld's revues were
transforming vaudeville into a Broadway mainstay,
Lydia Thompson-style burlesque shows were
moving into the neighborhood. A show from the
Progressive Burlesque Wheel (one of several burlesque touring organizations from the nineteenth
century) took over the defunct but venerable Daly's
Theatre on Broadway where a young Isadora
Duncan, among others, had performed. The *New
York Times* portrayed the reopening of this dead
theater as a tragedy, noting that "in the lobby,

The Sunshine Girls WERE A FEATURED ACT AT DALY'S THEATRE WHEN THE
PROGRESSIVE BURLESQUE WHEEL TOOK OVER THE VENUE. THEY WERE CONSIDERED
SCANDALOUS IN THE DAYS BEFORE ZIEGFELD UPPED THE ANTE ON STAGE NUDITY.

where once pictures of the greatest actors and actresses in the world hung . . . are the newcomers—burlesque kings and queens in fleshings and comedy 'make up.'" The whiff of class snobbery was in evidence as the reporter stated that the "mostly" male audience "had been forced to ask the way to Daly's Theatre when they heard that a real burlesque show was going to play there." The implication of the *Times* article is that burlesque shows are not theater; they merely take place in one. This reflects the historically and commonly held attitude about burlesque—an attitude that had necessitated the invention of vaudeville in the late nineteenth century. The marginal status of burlesque early in the revue era is also reflected in the police raids that constituted the bulk of burlesque press coverage. The charges were generally vague: "permitting the production of an immoral show"; the intriguing "improper lines and costumes"; and the old standby "indecency." The result was generally promises of reform followed by the announcement of victory by the forces of good. It was already a rather tired old tune by 1919 when Ziegfeld had introduced burlesque comedians and nude tableaux to his upscale audience.

The ascent of the increasingly explicit revues in the 1920s effectually blunted the once-shocking impact of burlesque queens and their traditional costume of fleshing-clad thighs. The Columbia Burlesque Wheel tried to draw an audience by advertising "clean" shows, but theater patrons rejected these. Other burlesque producers tried to stage their own revues, but the shows came across as cheap imitations, which they essentially were—audiences found "nothing to equal the audacity of Messrs. Ziegfeld . . . et al." Finally the burlesque show producers hit upon the solution, a way to outdo the revues: in a word, striptease.

By the mid 1920s, striptease had become the hot new act on burlesque stages, as evidenced by a new series of police raids and the complaints of the omnipresent New York Society for the Suppression of Vice. In 1927, theater critic J. Brooks Atkinson faintly noted the renewed interest in burlesque (of which he was not a fan)—quoting the nineteenth-century defense of burlesque that "it seems rather to be desired that the points of a fine woman should be somewhat better known and more thought of than they have been. They seem to me quite as important and, I think, that they are quite as interesting, as those of a fine horse"—but then dismisses the twentieth-century revival of the form on Broadway, saying that "[contemporary] burlesque . . . has lapsed into a leg show." Atkinson's opinion, however, was not universally held and, in the 1930s, burlesque could be derided, but not denied. It was succeeding where other theatrical ventures failed and the specialty dancer, that is to say, the stripteaser, had become burlesque itself. The ascent of striptease and the burlesque woman over the coy Ziegfeld-manufactured girl next door was in great part due to the efforts of a family of burlesque producing brothers named Minsky.

The story of the Minsky brothers is a classic, all-American one of immigrant success in the new world: from the Lower East Side to the Great White Way in less than thirty years. The Minskys—Abe, Billy, Herbert, and Morton—were the sons of a Jewish immigrant who had founded a successful retail business on the Lower East Side. The eldest brother, Abe, made the first foray into show business when he opened a nickelodeon called the Houston Street Hippodrome in 1908. He made a healthy profit showing films described as "dirty" by his brother Morton Minsky in the family's autobiography. The films were likely the tales of white slavery and morphine

SOME BURLESQUE PRODUCERS
THOUGHT "CLEAN" SHOWS WOULD
DRAW AUDIENCES BACK FROM THE
BROADWAY REVUES IN THE 1920S, SO
STARS SUCH AS *Mollie Williams*
KEPT THEIR TIGHTS ON LONG AFTER
THE ZIEGFELD GIRLS HAD DISPOSED
OF THEIRS. THE EXPERIMENT
PROVED A FAILURE.

addiction that were the top draws in those early days of film when the medium was too new to be policed by censors. Abe was forced to shut his business down when his father discovered the nature of the films he was showing. Fortunately for Abe, this discovery by his father was made three years after the business opened. Not too long after, Abe and younger brother Billy were able to get the family back into show business when their father allowed them to show (presumably unobjectionable) movies in the roof garden of the National Winter Garden theater on Houston Street, a theater that their father had helped to build in order to present Jewish plays to the Lower East Side community. The Minsky foray into the roof garden ran parallel to Florenz Ziegfeld's but, needless to say, a roof garden on the Lower East Side was far less respectable than a roof garden over a Broadway theater. And the content of Minsky productions would ultimately bear this out.

In 1914, Herbert Minsky joined the family business although World War I and increased competition in the movie business damaged the high profit margin the brothers had previously enjoyed at the National Winter Garden. They tried booking vaudeville acts in order to bring business back in, but found that they couldn't afford the better acts. Burlesque acts, with their innuendo-laden comedy and emphasis on girls, turned out to be cheaper. Cheaper still, the Minskys found, would be to start their own burlesque company using recycled burlesque scripts. Unfortunately, the scripts were so old that audiences found that they stank and stayed away in droves. Finally, Abe found the answer in his war experience—or rather, his experience of wartime Paris where he had visited the Folies-Bergère and the Moulin Rouge. After extrapolating (quite rightly) that other American service

men had been as dazzled and titillated by those shows as he had been, Abe suggested that they de-emphasize the comedy, use more girls, install theatrical lighting, and build a runway to bring the girls closer to the audience. Although the idea of an imitation of the Folies-Bergère, more girls, and halfway decent production values had already been used quite effectively by Ziegfeld, the runway was a real innovation. The Minskys were prepared to give their audience even more of what it wanted than Ziegfeld had, to deliver it more efficiently, and to give it to them at a lower price.

The Minsky streamlining of the glorified girl worked out well. Their first runway show, featuring six women in neck-to-toe pink tights and nothing else, sold out. Several good years followed for the Minskys. They promoted their shows to a fairly upscale clientele whom they reached through brother Billy Minsky's briefly held position as a society reporter for *The World* newspaper as well as through younger brothers Herbert and Morton's college friends. They also used the publicity brought by the occasional police raid, which they quickly discovered increased their profits. (Although they wisely took those profits and installed a warning system to avoid further prosecution—a switch that turned on a red light in view of the performers so they would know to change their act to the "Boston version.") The passage of prohibition boosted Minsky receipts further as the disreputable Lower East Side became a haven for speakeasies in a city whose populace had generally decided to ignore the ban on alcohol.

It was also around this time that Morton Minsky claims that his brothers sponsored the invention of striptease. In 1917, a Minsky theater soubrette named Mae Dix was coming to the end of her act in the overheated National Winter Garden theater.

In order to save on her laundry bill, she removed the detachable collar of her costume before giving an encore so it wouldn't be soiled. Fortunately, she executed this fastidious little maneuver in view of the audience who misunderstood her intentions entirely and began hooting for more. Ms. Dix, being no fool, went back out to the center of the stage and removed the detachable cuffs to her costume as well. She was further encouraged and opened the top few buttons on her bodice on her way off the stage. The Minsky brothers' contribution to her invention was to give her a ten dollar a week raise and ask her to make the innovation part of her act. The police busted them within weeks, providing valuable publicity to the Minskys and effectively launching their career in burlesque. Although women had removed their clothes on stage before, most notably as a part of the Salome dance, Mae Dix's performance marked the first time that had been done without any particular justification (other than to turn the crowd on).

Of course, there are others who claim to have "invented" the striptease. 1930s striptease star Ann Corio made a claim for dancer Hinda Wassau, who had insisted that she had unintentionally invented the striptease in a 1928 performance. Ms. Wassau was a chorus member of a burlesque show and the performer of the show's solo "shimmy" number. The shimmy was a popular evolution of Little Egypt's dance, done faster and set to jazz music. In order to avoid a time-consuming costume change, Ms. Wassau wore the beaded-fringe costume for the shimmy dance under her chorus costume. This system apparently failed one night when her chorus costume got hung on the beads of the costume underneath. At the bellowing behest of the stage manager, Ms. Wassau went out on stage with her chorus costume only halfway off. Fortunately, the shaking of the shimmy dance saved her performance:

Under the frantic vibrations of her anatomy, the outer costume started to come loose. So she removed as much of it as she could. The audience howled. She shimmied some more–and more of it came loose, and she removed that. By now the audience was with her all the way. At the climax of her number the costume came completely loose and she removed it. The applause at the end of her number was thunderous.

Corio herself acknowledged that this story is both dubious and a little too good to be true.

Morton Minsky can at least claim that his family's theaters invented the term *strip-tease.* Minsky publicists George Alabama Florida and Mike Goldreyer coined the word strip-tease in a 1920s press release to describe the acts at Minsky theaters. Whether the Minsky brothers presented the first striptease or not, they were certainly primarily responsible for promoting and popularizing it. At Minsky theaters, the names of striptease artists went above the names of comedians and other performers, a reversal of the policy of the nineteenth-century burlesque houses. The Minskys also added more and more solo dancers to their shows when they found that their specialty was the proven draw.

The 1920s were a period of rapid expansion for Minsky burlesque, which would become as much a brand name as the Ziegfeld *Follies.* In 1922, the brothers made their first attempt to establish themselves on Broadway when they leased the Park Theatre on Columbus Circle with the plan to produce cleaner shows. Reviews of the shows concluded that "the chief difference between the Minsky burlesques and the ordinary Broadway musical comedy is $2.20" but the theater still failed inside of six months. The Minskys concluded, as later revue producers would, that clean was not the

WHEN THE DEPRESSION
ENDED THE REVUES, ALL
OF THE GLORIFIED GIRLS
WERE OUT OF WORK. *Faith
Bacon* WAS ONE WHO
WENT FROM ZIEGFELD GIRL
IN THE 1920S TO MINSKY
GIRL IN THE 1930S.

Hinda Wassau WAS ONE OF SEVERAL WOMEN REPUTED TO HAVE INVENTED THE STRIPTEASE. SHE MAY OR MAY NOT HAVE, BUT HER STORY, THAT OF A HAPLESS INGÉNUE HITTING THE BIG TIME IN BURLESQUE, IS A GOOD ONE.

the proceedings were comical (Sumner attempted to show the court what exactly a dancer had been doing by performing the move himself on the stand) and the charges were dismissed. While the newspaper accounts do not detail exactly what was going on in Minsky shows to inspire so much attention from both audiences and censors, a 1925 *New Republic* article fully describes one skit at a National Winter Garden show, *Antony and Cleopatra*:

> [The piece] is particularly gratifying. "I'm dying. I'm dying," groans Antony. Whereupon all the rest of the company—Caesar, Cleopatra, the Roman soldiers and the beautiful Egyptian slave girls— break into a rousing shimmy to the refrain of "He's dying." . . . When he is dead Cleopatra applies to her breast what is described as a "vasp"—she falls prone over Antony's body, and Caesar places upon her posterior a wreath which he waters with a small watering pot.

way to go. In 1924, they opened a theater on 125th Street that featured more of what the Minsky name was becoming known for. There Billy Minsky staged a show satirizing the Ziegfeld-style girl show. Whereas a recent Broadway success had featured its chorus dressed in a costume of flowers who disrobed by throwing their costumes to the audience flower by flower, the Minskys had its chorus dressed as banana bunches, throwing their costumes off banana by banana. The police were inexplicably not amused and raided the show. The Minskys fought the charges, but graciously accepted the publicity. This strategy in dealing with censorship proved effective again when in 1925 the Minskys were raided by the terminally scandalized John Sumner. In the trial that ensued,

The *New Republic* reporter was unmistakably tickled with the goings on at the Minsky house. The *New Yorker* covered the brothers favorably as well, taking the Minsky name nationwide.

By the late 1920s, the Minskys went nationwide literally, taking over burlesque theaters outside New York City and building a touring circuit of their own as the nineteenth-century burlesque organizations like Progressive and Columbia went into bankruptcy. Finally, in 1931, Billy Minsky convinced a backer to buy Broadway's Republic Theatre and let him run it as a burlesque house. The Minskys had arrived on Broadway. The first Minsky burlesque Broadway show opened on February 12, 1931. A reader of the *New York Times* theater column could practically see critic J. Brooks Atkinson holding his nose as he reported that "the squealing and thumping on the shady side of Times Square these evenings may be taken to indicate that a burlesque show has settled down for the season in the Republic Theatre." By May of 1931, Billy Minsky was announcing plans for a thirty-theater burlesque circuit from New York to Chicago and, in July of that same year, he took over a second Broadway theater "which formerly played legitimate attractions." In 1932, Billy Minsky died, but his brothers continued to expand the business, leasing theaters in Brooklyn and New Jersey.

"Legitimate" Broadway theater operators were not pleased to have Minskys or low-priced burlesque shows as neighbors. They and Broadway real estate owners made their feelings known to New York City elected officials. What followed was a series of legal skirmishes between the Minskys and New York City's theater License Commissioners. In October 1933, License Commissioner Sidney S. Levine demanded that the female cast of Minsky shows be "decently clad" forthwith. Herbert Minsky responded that there was no indecency in his theater's "classical" presentation. In 1935, another License Commissioner, Paul Moss, had a Minsky show raided and arrested three dancers on charges of "giving an indecent performance." Moss followed this with the suspension of Minsky's theater license for the Republic Theatre. In the ensuing court fight, the Minskys were victorious. The judge ruled that the city's License Commissioners had no power to revoke a license without an obscenity conviction. Emboldened by the decision, Minsky brothers Herbert and Morton decided to take burlesque upscale. In 1936, they opened Minsky's Oriental at 51st Street and groomed themselves as the second coming of Ziegfeld, presenting something even better than the glorified girl.

That something better was, of course, a stripteaser. She was the Minskys's main attraction, bringing police and audiences to burlesque theaters again and again. She was the heir of Little Egypt, Isadora Duncan, Ruth St. Denis, and Maud Allan and, unlike the Cinderellas of Ziegfeld's chorus, she was her own creation. Lower-class girls with dreams of show biz and experienced vaudeville performers in need of a good gig to ride out the Great Depression had found their niche. In the loosened strictures of burlesque, these dancers set the chaste nude of the tableau vivant into sudden motion. The Minskys named the act, but the women were the show—and the audience would follow them to any theater.

The first and greatest of the striptease stars was Gypsy Rose Lee. Through her own ambition and hard work, she did as much to popularize the striptease as all the burlesque publicity men put together. Gypsy Rose Lee literally grew up in vaudeville theaters, playing secondary roles to her younger, cuter sister who was billed as Dainty June. Under the management of her mother, Lee and her sister toured with a troupe of child performers through small-time regional vaudeville houses and then on big-time stages until no one in the group could really be called "Dainty." At age thirteen June eloped, leaving fifteen-year-old Lee with their domineering mother at the onset of the Great Depression. Lee's mother decided to build a new act centered on Lee and started to look for bookings. They went to a few nightclubs but found gigs few and far between—as did most vaudevillians at the end of the 1920s. Eventually, tight finances forced them to accept a booking at a burlesque theater (which Lee's mother considered a step down from their previous vaudeville success). According to her autobiography, Lee was immediately intrigued by

IT'S HARD TO SAY WHICH ONE
MADE THE OTHER FAMOUS,
BUT *Gypsy Rose Lee* AND THE
ACT OF STRIPTEASE REMAIN
INEXTRICABLY LINKED.

In the parlance of burlesque producers, *Margie Hart* "played strong." The key element of her act was that she supposedly performed without a g-string. Ironically, because she never actually removed her skirt—only shifted it strategically—she was able to continue performing in New York City even as striptease became increasingly regulated.

the world of burlesque. The world of burlesque must have been intrigued with her too, as she was recruited into a comedy skit on her first day. Lee continued in burlesque, at first as the leader of her own vaudeville-style act where she sang and danced. After some experience on the circuit, she developed a striptease act in order to replace a burlesque show lead. She did so well that before the season was over she got a telegram from Billy Minsky inviting her to come be a headliner at the Republic Theatre in 1931.

Although Lee tells a great story in her autobiography, it is probably not entirely accurate. Lee herself acknowledged later in life that she was not as concerned with a true story as she was with a good one. The truth was that she was a driven performer who wanted to be the star of the show, even if the show was in burlesque. She went to work for Billy Minsky as an experienced vaudevillian, not as the wide-eyed and guileless girl she describes in her autobiography. Morton Minsky even described her as a grasping, pretentious publicity hound. Whatever the reality, it was no mere happy accident that Lee was the first stripteaser to get top billing at the Republic Theatre. It was an expression of her naked ambition. She worked hard to be more than a run-of-the-mill stripteaser, making her act into part comedy routine and addressing her audience directly. In one shtick, she slowly removed her clothes as she narrated what really went on in the mind of a stripteaser. Lee's wit, stunning beauty, and the polish of her act, not to mention her vigorous self-promotion, made her a success in New York City. She hoped she would move from burlesque into one of the revues, but that didn't happen right away. Instead, Lee spent the 1930s making her and the striptease act famous in burlesque theaters. In 1936, she was able to make the leap that few burlesque

stars could make—into legitimate theater as a star of the revived Ziegfeld *Follies.* The arc of her career would inspire other burlesque stars to embellish their acts with vaudeville tricks and gimmicks.

Margie Hart, who started working for the Minskys in 1934, was not the publicity hound that Gypsy Rose Lee was. Still, she managed to draw plenty of attention, particularly with her reputation for performing without a g-string. Whether or not that reputation was justified is difficult to establish since none of the historians of the Minsky era will definitively state that she was completely naked. The question was probably academic for anyone without a front row seat anyway. Hart made two major contributions to striptease. The first was to call upon H. L. Mencken to provide her with a term for her profession. He dubbed her an *ecdysiast* from the Greek meaning "to molt" or "to shed," a term that stuck around into the 1950s. Her second contribution was to dispense with the "strip" part of the striptease. Instead, according to Morton Minsky, she wore costumes that

> [C]onsisted of narrow strips of silk that hung from the waist down the front and back with the sides bare. . . . In this way she could expose her legs by intimately flicking the protective slips of silk back and forth with a casual twist of her fingers. . . . It was something that the censors had trouble dealing with since she was not taking the dress off.

Hart also gained a measure of notoriety for her conflict with another stripteaser, Rose la Rose, who apparently dressed and performed in a way that too strongly resembled Hart's style. This kind of copycatting was taboo in the somewhat small world of burlesque theaters. The conflict came to a head when Hart had plastic surgery on her nose and

The Minsky's first Broadway theater.

Rose followed suit soon after. Having had enough, Hart took a swing at Rose backstage at a Brooklyn burlesque theater and effectively dispensed with the problem of the too-similar nose. Rose was out of work for a month.

Another famous stripteaser who didn't actually strip was Georgia Southern. Southern had gotten her showbiz start dancing in an act with her uncle in vaudeville. Her act in burlesque consisted of a fast, ferocious, hip-shaking dance to a tune called "Hold That Tiger." Southern signed with the Minskys around 1931 and one year later revealed that she was only fourteen and had signed her contract at age thirteen. The Minskys decided to keep this quiet since Southern had already made herself a top attraction at the Republic.

The last of the big Minsky burlesque stars was Ann Corio. She had started in show business at age fifteen as part of a touring vaudeville chorus, but had left the show within two weeks from homesickness. When she later took a job in a burlesque show, she said she had thought burlesque was just another form of vaudeville. She ascended from the chorus to become a stripteaser and was soon after offered a role in Earl Carroll's *Vanities* for half the pay she was making in burlesque. She decided to stay with the money. Corio's act was the opposite of Margie Hart's. Instead of playing strong (burlesque slang for a striptease that relied on blatant flashes of breasts, buttocks, and genitals), she played coy and innocent, never showing that much skin. She remained a draw in burlesque throughout the 1930s, although some of her contemporaries suggested at the time that this was more a result of her marriage to a burlesque producer than to her talent.

What Corio and most of the other stars had in common was an act or gimmick. They didn't just take off their clothes. They made it fun. And they made good copy. 1930s newspapers and magazines loved striptease and burlesque, and stripteasers and burlesque theaters loved publicity. For a good part of the 1930s, burlesque and striptease shows were the only blockbusters on Broadway. But the drummers' rim shots punctuating burlesque bump and grind dances were not music to the ears of legitimate Broadway producers. And the fun was about to stop.

The burlesque theaters, Minsky-owned and otherwise, were harassed by appointed and unappointed censors throughout the 1930s. 1933 License Commissioner James F. Geraghty ordered, "all stripping acts were to be eliminated." License Commissioner Levine issued summonses for indecency. License Commissioner Moss proposed to clean up dance halls, poolrooms, and the stage. The reformers were only incrementally successful. In 1934, Moss effected the removal of burlesque theater runways. He also tried to deny a license to an additional burlesque theater on Broadway, but the courts sided once again with the burlesque producers and it seemed, at least to burlesque producers, that they always would.

That hopeful thinking abruptly ended in a case that stemmed from a complaint brought by, who else, John S. Sumner of the New York Society for the Suppression of Vice against a performance at Abe Minsky's Gotham Theatre at East 125th Street on August 27, 1936. After five hours of testimony on April 8, 1937, the performers and the theater manager were found guilty of giving an indecent performance. The *New York Times* noted that, "The conviction was looked on as spelling the doom of the Minsky type of 'living art' in burlesque theatres in this city, to which Mayor La Guardia, Police Commissioner Valentine and License Commissioner Moss have been hostile."

Rose La Rose WAS BEST KNOWN IN THE BURLESQUE WORLD AS THE NEMESIS OF MINSKY STAR MARGIE HART. HER ACT WAS NOTABLY SIMILAR TO HART'S AND SHE EVEN GOT A NOSE JOB IMMEDIATELY FOLLOWING HART'S OWN RHINOPLASTY. HART RESPONDED BY PUNCHING LA ROSE IN THE FACE WHEN THEY FOUND THEMSELVES TOGETHER BACKSTAGE. FORTUNATELY, LA ROSE WAS FULLY RECOVERED BY THE TIME SHE POSED FOR THIS 1941 PHOTO.

The net paid circulation
for March exceeded
Daily --- 1,650,000
Sunday - 3,100,000

DAILY NEWS

NEW YORK'S PICTURE NEWSPAPER

Copyright 1937 by News Syndicate Co. Inc. Reg. U.S Pat. Off.

Entered as 2nd class matter, Post Office, New York, N. Y.

★★★★
FINAL

Vol. 18. No. 264   New York, Friday, April 30, 1937*   72 Main + 8 Manhattan Pages   2 Cents IN CITY LIMITS | 3 CEN Elsewh

SHOW RAIDS NET 11 GIRLS

—Story on Page 3

Strip-tease artists, arrested in raids on Brooklyn burlesque theatres last night, are booked at the Poplar St. police station. Eleven girls, three managers and two assistant managers were hustled off to jail. —Story p. 3.

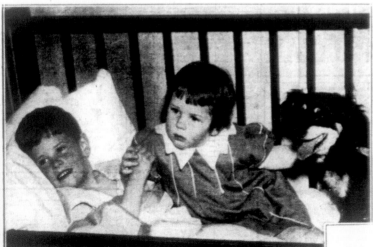

They Owe Their Lives to Dog

Mired to their armpits in mud of Kisena Park, Flushing, swamps, Marilyn Johnson, 3, and Kenneth Garrison, 5, were saved by Marilyn's mongrel pup, Peggy. Dog, shown with children, barked until help came.

Burlesque Bars Her

While Peggy Garcia (above) waited in D. A.'s ofice to learn if she'll be tried on charge of trying to shake down Dave Rubinoff, burlesque men pointed out she's barred from burlesque.

Their assessment was correct . . . sort of. Legal wrangling ensued for about a month following the conviction. License Commissioner Moss held hearings. According to the *Times*, at them,

> A stream of witnesses, most of them affiliated with Catholic organizations, described perform-ances . . . [detailing] the appearance, clothing, actions and lines of the actors and actresses. . . . At one point, Mr. Moss decided that the "strip-tease" act had been described often enough for the purposes of the record.

Reformers suggested the "salacious performances in burlesque" were contributing to a wave of sex crimes in New York. One attorney suggested that while the License Commissioner could not revoke all burlesque licenses at will, he could refuse renewals. The representatives of burlesque theaters declined to present a defense. Abe Minsky became so hostile at the hearing that he had to be escorted out of the building. Days later, Herbert and Morton Minsky announced that they would be pulling out of burlesque production and would instead begin producing entertainment "on the revue type." Ultimately, there were no more raids or arrests. Burlesque went down at the stroke of a pen when Moss simply refused to renew burlesque theater licenses when they expired on May 1, 1937, stating, "I am satisfied that the proof before me clearly indi-cates that the type of performance, the language used, the display of nudity are coarse, vulgar and lewd and endanger public morality in the welfare of the community and are a disgrace to the people of the City of New York." He also wrote a policy that no entertainment called "burlesque" or advertised with the name "Minsky" could be licensed in New York. Burlesque, and by extension striptease, was banned in New York City.

Except that it wasn't. Continuing coverage of the adventures of License Commissioner Moss by the *New York Times* reveals that he continued to police the same burlesque theaters, managers, and performers who now put on "variety-revue pro-grams" called "Follies" (no doubt causing Florenz Ziegfeld Jr. to roll over in his grave). The burlesque managers did continue to sue to get the word "burlesque" back, but to no avail. Still, if burlesque had been stopped, striptease had not. Even avowed burlesque foe J. Brooks Atkinson had to admit:

> The striptease is as much a part of American cul-ture as the hot-dog and hamburger. The American sense of humor has handled the striptease more intelligently than the moralists. Ann Corio and Margie Hart are as much a part of show business as the circus.
>
> And Gypsy Rose Lee, who can strip from the inside out, as she did at the World's Fair, is a national figure in more ways than one, admired for her wit and intelligence as much as her stage hocus-pocus.

And this was undeniably so. The striptease suppos-edly banned in New York City in 1937 had simply found another stage. ✩

---

opposite: On April 30, 1937, the Minskys and other burlesque producers learned from the headlines of *The Daily News* that there was such a thing as bad publicity. The official ban on burlesque in New York City was in effect the following day.

CLASSIC STRIPTEASE

or

BIG NAMES, BIGGER BREASTS

Gypsy Rose Lee STILL DOING HER
STRIPTEASE ACT IN THE EARLY 1950S.

opposite: **Sally Rand** CONSIDERED
HERSELF A CABARET ACT, NOT A
STRIPTEASER . . . BUT THE DISTINC-
TION WOULD SEEM TO BE ACADEMIC.
SHE NEVER STRIPPED OFF ANY
CLOTHES, BUT HER PERFORMANCES,
SUCH AS THE BUBBLE DANCE SHOWN
HERE, WERE ALL ABOUT THE TEASE.
HER GIMMICKS WERE WIDELY IMI-
TATED ON THE STRIPTEASE CIRCUIT.

The fatal force, however, was striptease. It grew to be almost the sole feature of the entertainment. First one stripper came on, and then another and still another. The comics had brief moments and limited attention. The humor was gone. Loud speakers displaced straight men. The entertainment dwindled to what *Variety* called "epileptics"—sex-starved men whose only physical experience was limited to abnormal concentration on bodies they could see but never know.

—Bernard Sobel from *A Pictorial History of Burlesque*, 1956

stages turned out not to be the end but instead the beginning of its proliferation in other venues. In 1939, the 1920s-style revue—without which the act of being nude on a stage would have been undefendable—was making a comeback as George White announced plans to stage another *Scandals*. It would, of course, feature:

> Girls, very young and fast dancers, [doing] pretty
> much the same thing that all "Scandals" ensem-
> bles have always done against the usual back-
> grounds, with and without costumes. This being
> August, they were working mostly without. They
> are, by turn, Hawaiians, Spanish, coquettes,
> cocottes and nudes.

With burlesque gone, it seemed it would be like the 1920s all over again. White would continue to stage his revues into the 1940s and they would be presented not only on Broadway, but also on the stages of what would become striptease's new home into the 1950s, the grand-scale nightclub.

As producer-driven revues made a comeback in the 1940s, the striptease act was in somewhat of a state of flux. Following the 1937 ban on burlesque in New York City, several other cities instituted similar censorship. The offending act of striptease had been identified as the main draw of burlesque, so the theaters that featured burlesque shows were singled out for special regulation. This put the striptease in danger of becoming a performance without a stage. Striptease performers would have to take action if they wanted to survive. Former Ziegfeld girl and latter-day Minskyite Faith Bacon was a haphazard pioneer of preservation as she attempted to get press coverage for her appearance at the 1939 World's Fair. The *New York Times* reports:

At 1:10 Miss Bacon came out on Park Avenue, her translucent chiffon gown billowing about her bare thighs. In one hand she held bits of apple that she believed would soothe the skittish 200-pound fawn tugging at a chain in her other hand. In a few minutes nearly 100 persons were forming a circle about the thoroughly frightened animal.

Struggling desperately, the animal was led, carried and tugged the length of the block to Thirty-ninth Street. There, bleeding slightly, it lay down to rest while the publicity men scanned the horizon hopefully for a radio car, and Miss Bacon regarded her toenails whose crimson shade seemed to clash with the simple Grecian sandals.

After ten minutes two radio cars pulled up and four patrolmen surrounded Miss Bacon and her fawn. One of them muttered, "World's Fair special"; the others nodded wisely and decided to notify their sergeant before taking any action.

Bacon was arrested and met with the exclamation "What in the name of thunderation is this!" by the desk sergeant before being fined $500 and scolded by the ASPCA. Her act at the Fair was very well attended.

Burlesque houses struggled on in New York during the early 1940s. In order to comply with the letter of the law, the Republic Theatre and other Broadway burlesque houses "agreed to drop the word 'burlesque' when Mayor LaGuardia permitted them to reopen with variety-revue programs, many of which [were] called 'Follies.'" This compromise was only in effect until 1942 when burlesque theater licenses were again denied on the grounds that they presented "indecent and immoral shows." Burlesque producers cried censorship, but Mayor LaGuardia dismissively responded:

In the late 1930s and the 1940s, revues that had been on Broadway found a home in nightclubs. *Earl Carroll's Vanities* franchise was able to survive this way even as Carroll himself recovered from bankruptcy. These trading cards, which could be purchased from vending machines, show early 1940s *Vanities* girls.

I challenge any of the partisans of "G-string" morality who are responsible for raising the red herring of censorship in this case to state publicly that the endless debauches in undressing which characterized the performances given by the petitioner in this case, and by its fellow operators, were not indecent and obscene.

The burlesque producers fought the ruling of the courts with support from the League of New York Theatres, the Actors Equity Association, the Authors League of America, the Dramaticists Guild, the Radio Writers Guild, and several labor unions, but they lost again. The burlesque houses that managed to survive outside of New York City were much harassed into the 1940s. Due to the constant scrutiny of moralists, they were unable to put on a good, scandalous show. Consequently, no tony *New Yorker* scribes wanted to go to burlesque houses anymore. By the late 1940s, burlesque stripteasers were getting a little long in the tooth and burlesque houses seemed like a very old-fashioned entertainment. But the desire to see "something you can't get at home" was as strong as ever. If the climate for striptease was unfavorable in some cities, the performers took the show on the road. Before anyone realized, that something you couldn't get at home was coming to hometown America.

The 1939 World's Fair in Queens, New York, was one of the first nonburlesque venues to host the star stripteasers in their exodus out of burlesque houses. Gypsy Rose Lee was able to perform there without objection. Also featured were Rosita Royce, who appeared dressed only in her trained doves; Faith Bacon, who performed without her fawn; and Tirza, who "bathed" for the audience in a wine bath. Some impresarios at the Fair also attempted to organize a "Miss Nude of the World's Fair 1939," but were met with resistance and then arrest by the Sheriff in charge. The qualified success of striptease at the World's Fair midway revealed a market for nationally known stripteasers on carnival midways. Gypsy Rose Lee put together an "American Beauties" revue and performed at carnivals and fairs across the United States, as did other stripteasers who had gained fame during the Minsky era. In this way, the formerly urban phenomenon of striptease expanded into the heartland of America.

The struggling burlesque houses and various carnival midways aside, the most important venue for the striptease turned out to be one that was already entrenched across the nation in the 1940s—the nightclub. As burlesque had boomed in 1930s New York, small nightclubs were becoming an established part of the entertainment world. They were the descendants of the cabaret restaurants of the 1910s that had been driven underground to become speakeasies in the 1920s. As speakeasies, the venues had been profitable and sometimes glamorous, but not particularly reputable. Following the repeal of the ban on alcohol, speakeasies became nightclubs hosting the same kinds of acts that had been featured in revues, including chorus girls, dancers of all kinds, singers, and comedians. The newly popular stripteasers were brought into the mix as well. In 1931, nightclubs were still a dubious enterprise, considered little more than fleecing stations for tourists still in search of the Roaring Twenties. Since they had become the haunts of low-level criminals during prohibition, instances of fraud were not uncommon, as was shrilly reported by the ever-vigilant New York Society for the Suppression of Vice:

THE BURLESQUE SHOWS POPULARIZED BY THE MINSKYS IN THE 1930S CONTINUED INTO THE 1940S ON TOURING CIRCUITS DEVELOPED BY THE MINSKYS AND OTHER BURLESQUE MANAGERS. UNFORTUNATELY, WHATEVER MAGIC THERE HAD BEEN THAT MADE STRIPTEASERS SUCH AS GYPSY ROSE LEE INTO NATIONAL CELEBRITIES WAS LESS IN EVIDENCE. IN THIS SERIES OF POSTCARDS, LOWER PRODUCTION VALUES AND A LESSER DEGREE OF SELECTIVITY SEEM TO BE THE ORDER OF THE DAY IN 1940S BURLESQUE. *Jeanne Joyce* HAS A KILLER BODY, BUT A CROOKED SMILE. *Lucrezia Borgia* IS LESS THAN GRACEFULLY DRAPED AROUND HER LAMPPOST SET PIECE. THE RHINESTONES *Marcella* WEARS AROUND HER NECK DO NOT COMPLETELY OBSCURE ITS SAG. THE THICK SHINE OF MAKE UP ON *Babs Mitchell* SUGGESTS SHE MIGHT BE TRYING TO HIDE HER AGE. *Ellye Monroe* SEEMS YOUNG ENOUGH, BUT MADE MORE OF GANGLY ANGLES THAN SENSUOUS CURVES. ONLY *Ann Perri* SEEMS TO OFFER THE FULL PACKAGE OF BODY, FACE, AND GRACE. BUT STILL, THEY ALL APPEAR TO BE ONLY RETREADS OF ACTS FROM THE 1930S. 1950S STRIPTEASE WOULD NEED TO OFFER SOMETHING MORE TO SURVIVE.

ONCE REVUES WERE TOO COSTLY AND BURLESQUE
WAS BANNED, SMALL-SCALE FLOOR SHOWS FOUND A
HOME IN NIGHTCLUBS ACROSS THE UNITED STATES.

NIGHTCLUBS HAD BEEN BORN AS CABARETS IN THE 1900S AND MULTIPLIED AS SPEAKEASIES DURING THE PROHIBITION ERA. WHEN BUR-
LESQUE WAS BANNED IN NEW YORK CITY (AND WAS UNDER ATTACK BY CENSORS IN OTHER CITIES), STRIPTEASERS QUIETLY DISPERSED
INTO THE CRAMPED CONFINES OF THE NIGHTCLUB THAT EVENTUALLY REDUCED THEIR STAGE SHOWS TO ONLY THE BARE ESSENTIALS.

[When nightclubs are] permit[ted] to remain open until 3 A.M. . . . [t]he consequence is that in places licensed by the city of New York, foolish people on the one hand, and the most desperate crooks on the other, are enabled to congregate and many a crime of fraud or violence has been committed or concocted in these malodorous places.

Though probably an exaggeration, the perceived danger of nightclubs provided an excuse for reforms that allowed the city to regain some control over clubs that had been unpoliced in the 1920s. To that end, the New York City Police Department was given power over licensing nightclubs and cabarets; rules were established prohibiting hostesses from circulating among patrons; owners, operators, and managers were finger-printed; known criminals were denied entry; and nightclub employees were subject to questioning by police. Within two years, the 1931 reforms seemed to have served their purpose as nightclubs were being discussed as entertainment venues, rather than the sites of gangland violence. Dancers previously employed in revues began to be booked into the cleaned-up nightclubs. By 1934, the nightclub curfew was extended to 4:00 A.M. and license fees were raised from $100 to $150. This move was expected to produce $200,000 in revenue for the depression-strapped city, which bought the nightclubs a lot of good will at city hall. By 1936, nightclubs were hosting scaled-back versions of the Broadway revues with titles like *Paradise Parade of 1936* and *Folies de Femmes.* The nightclub's popularity was by no means limited to

New York City or even to urban areas. Supper clubs with stage entertainment were springing up in mid-size cities and roadhouses were hosting a bawdy good time in rural areas. The trend was noted with approval as a sign that the Great Depression was lifting and,

The dollar [was] rolling freely again not only in New York's resorts but in the familiar gathering places of night life from Boston to Hollywood. A regular chain of elaborate "casinos," provided with large revue units sent out intact from one of Broadway's most sumptuous cabarets, [was] being welded into the shape of a popular national institution.

And the entertainment at nightclubs? The huge production numbers were a well-publicized feature of the most upscale nightclubs, but,

By far the most persistent type of after-dark club, so far as numbers is concerned, is the intimate, generally rowdy and innately fly-by-night affair of which several dozen are scattered about the city. . . .

Noisy and completely informal, they catch most of the late-night trade of assorted tourists who still mean to paint the town red, society slummers, college kids stomping to swing music, sporting wiseacres and just plain owls. Entertainment is fast and flashy—hot-cha singers, fan dancers, strip-tease artists and the like—and acknowledges few inhibitions.

Striptease was already immensely popular at nightclubs even before Moss's ban on burlesque. One club, designed by one of the most popular decorators of themed nightclubs in the 1930s, was planning to present striptease exclusively. The decor was described as follows:

The staircase to the club proper has legs for a balustrade. The walls of the large room are decorated with famous nudes: Eve, Botticelli's Venus, Lady Godiva, the Fan Dancer, the Bubble Dancer. The bar is a bedstead. The back is a lavish French canopy; the riser is quilted in satin. The cashier's seat is arranged so that the girl will look as though she's sitting up in bed. She will wear a Bergdorf-Goodman negligee and have satin pillows at her back. The bartenders will be uniformed in Chavez pajamas. The walls of the foyer will be covered with "solid and genuine ermine tails."

Unfortunately for the history of kitsch, that striptease club never opened. Right after the Moss ban, striptease in the clubs was attacked as well, with police stating that there would be "no double standard" for nightclubs. The violations listed by the police in their rebuke to nightclubs confirm that the striptease they were hosting was not far from what was on the burlesque stages:

Staff found indecency and nudity in four parts of the French Casino's floor show—the champagne bottle scene, the bird act, the clam beach scene and the skit entitled "Paris of 1937."

At the Cotton Club the dancing by the performers was found objectionably suggestive and indecent by the police. . . .

The Hollywood Restaurant was charged with permitting girl dancers to appear on the floor nude from the waist up and placarding the lobby of the establishment with suggestive photographs. . . .

At the Harlem Uproar fault was found with "Faulty Bare Facts," a skit, a veil dance by a girl who, after discarding the veil, is scantily clad, and suggestive songs by the master of ceremonies.

By the 1950s, New York City stripteasers were fully established in the city's nightclubs, which maintained a much lower profile than the Broadway burlesque houses had. The clubs were slightly off the beaten track, located mostly on West 53rd Street and West 3rd Street, and were more "intimate" than the full-scale theaters that had featured burlesque, as can be seen in this photo of *Venus LaDoll* performing at Club Savannah on West 3rd Street.

MICHAEL P. IANNUCCI

presents

ANN CORIO

IN

THIS WAS BURLESQUE

Despite the clear duplication of the burlesque striptease on nightclub stages, the "no double standard" announcement proved to be false. The lower profile and high tax paying nightclubs in New York City absorbed and supported the striptease act throughout the 1940s. They were occasionally busted by the police, but never closed for long. This development in nightclub culture in New York City was paralleled in other cities, creating a nationwide touring circuit for striptease dancers. These dancers, having been forcibly separated from burlesque comedians and skits by the ban on burlesque, now took center stage.

By the 1950s, there were numerous other young women earning livings as stripteasers. It seemed to be a growth industry. Accounts of 1950s striptease describe the elaborate sets and acts that drew audiences to nightclubs. Blaze Fury's stage act featured a large devil's head prop that provided her with a spotlight out of one of its eyes. She had another act where she did a bump and grind against a prop palm tree causing it to "explode" in a burst of flash powder provided by a stagehand. Stripper Ricki Corvette's act, designed "especially for clubs," involved a shower in a bubble-making machine and a stage exit "wearing only a mink." World's Fair performer Tirza updated her act for the 1950s with a new wine bath that had more power—variable settings for the spray included a stream setting, a spray setting, a dry-ice mist, and a bubble setting—and four mirrors at the back and sides. Because of the elaborate needs of her set, Tirza had trouble with the theatrical unions and solved them by becoming a licensed plumber and member of the American Federation of Labor.

1930s stripteasers Gypsy Rose Lee and Ann Corio continued to be presences on the American striptease scene through the 1950s. Lee had the most varied career. After her stint as a star of *Ziegfeld Follies of 1936,* she achieved the elusive dream of all star-struck vaudevillians: a Hollywood contract. Lee went to Hollywood in 1937 to be a 20th Century Fox player, but not without the stigma that would effectively sink her movie career. The Hays office, "being further embarrassed by the migration to Hollywood of the strip-tease artists," insisted that the studio not use Lee's name or notoriety in promoting her. Consequently, Lee was reinvented as a subdued Hollywood star under her real name, Louise Hovick. Hovick was not the star Lee was and her movies were unremarkable and not particularly profitable. That was the end of Lee's studio career. She did make a few "B" movies later in life, but never achieved big-time movie stardom. Ultimately, that wouldn't be necessary as the notoriety Lee had cultivated as a stripteaser sustained her for the rest of her life. She parlayed it into a career as author of a mystery novel (*The G-String Murders*), the host of a radio quiz show, and a member of multiple television show panels. She also wrote an autobiography that became the basis for a Broadway musical and then a movie. She also continued in striptease as a performer and as the impresario of her own touring show. At the end of her life, she even managed to get her own talk show that was on television for two years. Lee was also important to 1950s striptease as an inspiration—hers was the name dropped both by top stars (as a first idol) and by nightclub managers who were recruiting new performers (as an example of the kind of fame to be had in the field of striptease).

IN 1937 *Gypsy Rose Lee* COVERED
UP AND BECAME *Louise Hovick*,
20TH CENTURY FOX CONTRACT
PLAYER. THE TRANSFORMATION
DIDN'T TAKE.

MANY BURLESQUE STARS
WENT INTO THE BUSINESS
WITH DREAMS OF BIGGER
FAME IN LEGITIMATE SHOW
BIZ. FEW ACHIEVED THEM.
Ann Corio AT LEAST MAN-
AGED B-MOVIE STARDOM IN
ROLES THAT SHOWCASED
HER SKIMPY COSTUMES.

Ann Corio also continued her career as a stripteaser into the 1950s. After the New York City burlesque ban, she toured with shows in the burlesque theaters of cities where the form had not been banned. She then spent several years in Hollywood as a "B" movie queen. Her films had unfinished scripts, shaky finances, and called on her to wear tiny costumes, but they were a good living. In 1960, Corio achieved the previously impossible: she brought burlesque back to New York City. With author Joseph DiMona, she put together a 1930s style burlesque show, complete with broad comedy, a mildly inept chorus line, and striptease. Their show, *This Was Burlesque,* premiered at a Lower East Side theater in 1960 and was on Broadway in three-years time. A profitable tour of the show followed and Corio topped off the triumph with her own history of burlesque, published in 1968.

In addition to Lee, Corio, and other Minsky-era stars, a crop of new stripteasers also appeared in the 1950s. One of the most well known was Blaze Starr. Born Fannie Belle Fleming, granddaughter of a twelve-toed West Virginia moonshiner, Starr left her home at age fifteen in search of a good job. She had found work as a waitress, first in a beer hall and then in a donut shop, when a customer, Red Snyder, offered to help her get into show business. The following day, sixteen-year-old Starr found herself singing onstage in a cowgirl outfit with a low cut top and loving it. Unfortunately, the "cowboy" with whom she was singing did not love the competition for audience attention and booted her from his act. Her benefactor, Snyder, bought her a new dress and convinced her that she should strip

instead. Starr agreed and premiered her striptease the next night. Afterwards, Snyder took her to what he said would be a party and, in her words, "commenced lollygagging all over [her]." Starr escaped Snyder and her first striptease job through a bathroom window, but remained intrigued with the idea of becoming a stripper. She practiced routines in her boarding house room and then made her way to Baltimore (which she had heard was a striptease mecca) to get a job at the Two O'Clock Club.

After a few years of work and some good publicity stunts, including traveling with a panther she was trying to train to remove her clothes, Starr became a striptease headliner. When her panther escaped and had to be turned over to animal control, she developed a new act where she "would lie down on a red shag carpet and pretend to *be* a panther, screaming and crawling all over the carpet." This particular shtick must have been affecting because it got her arrested in Philadelphia. Later, Starr developed inventive props for her striptease. Her most famous was her combustible couch–a second-hand settee that she reupholstered in red velvet and rigged with chemical smoke, a blaze-colored piece of Chinese silk, and a fan that would "ignite" the couch at the climax of her performance. She later added flickering colored lights to the base of the couch to intensify the effect. Starr's ingenuity and notoriety took her to New Orleans in 1959 where she began stripping at Sho-Bar and met Louisiana governor Earl Long. Governor Long was a notorious figure on Bourbon Street, known to like a good time and not to mind getting any bad publicity over it. He and Starr started an affair, which eventually contributed to Long's commitment to a mental institution by his

---

*opposite: **Blaze Starr** WAS HOTTER THAN A TWO-DOLLAR PISTOL, BUT THE REAL SECRET OF HER SUCCESS WAS HER INVENTIVE USE OF GIMMICKS FROM TWIRLING TASSELS TO FLAMING COUCHES.*

Tempest Storm SHOWCASING WHAT
DEAN MARTIN AND JERRY LEWIS
CALLED THE "TWO BIGGEST PROPS
IN HOLLYWOOD."

wife and family. After Long's death, Starr returned to Baltimore and became the owner of the Two O'Clock Club, performing there and managing the club into the 1970s.

Tempest Storm was another of the 1950s striptease headliners. She shared a rural background with Blaze Starr, but took a different route to her striptease career. At age fourteen, she married a soldier in order to escape her abusive stepfather. Once safely away, she divorced her first husband and moved to Macon, Georgia, for a job and a room in a boarding house. There she decided she wanted to go to Hollywood and become a star. She married again in order to catch a ride as far west as Fort Benning, Georgia. She abandoned her second husband and took a job at a hosiery factory until she met a man who offered her a ride to California. Once in California, Storm found her way to Hollywood proper as a waitress. A customer at the bar where she worked suggested to Storm that she get into burlesque—still legal and thriving in Hollywood. In her autobiography, Storm claims she was concerned that her breasts were too large for burlesque, but gave it a try anyway. She ended up getting a job at The Follies Theater in the chorus and then quickly becoming a stripteaser.

Storm didn't have any gimmick or special attraction to her other than her name and her spectacular breasts, which were especially impressive in the pre-silicone era. At the height of her 1950s fame, she even received an award at an Oscars parody from Jerry Lewis and Dean Martin for having the "two biggest props in Hollywood." Storm augmented her fame with several high profile relationships, including affairs with Mickey Rooney, Sammy Davis Jr., Nat King Cole, John F. Kennedy, Vic Damone, Trini Lopez, Engelbert Humperdinck, and a young Elvis Presley. Storm's

career continued beyond the 1950s and, in 1973, she became the first stripteaser to ever perform at Carnegie Hall. In the 1980s, she headlined burlesque revival shows such as *Sugar Daddy* and *Hot and Stormy.*

While Blaze Starr and Tempest Storm appealed to the taste for the top heavy, which was one of the distinguishing features of 1950s striptease, Lili St. Cyr took a different tack. She did a high-class striptease. She was an extremely polished performer and a trained dancer. Her physical ability separated her from the busty and sometimes zaftig stars who had a very limited repertoire of dance moves. In many ways, she was a throw-back to the most polished of the 1930s stripteasers and the Ziegfeld showgirl—she didn't gain publicity through a raucous private life, but instead made her reputation on her revue-style shows that featured expensive sets and elaborate costumes. She had routines based on Salome, the opera *Carmen,* and *The Picture of Dorian Gray.* She also had an act where she portrayed a bride on her wedding night changing from a veil, to blue underthings, to black negligee, and then to bubbles as she bathed in a glass-walled tub. For that act, she earned $5,000 per week in a Las Vegas nightclub.

Top stars Storm, Starr, and St. Cyr were the marquee names of the nightclub shows centered on striptease. Their acts were the climax of shows that featured other, lesser-known stripteasers, comedy acts, and the last vestiges of the vaudeville acts. The 1953 film *A Night in Hollywood* offers a portrayal of the 1950s nightclub striptease show. The film opens with an older woman singing what she called the "Hollywood news" in rhyme and a mangled Cuban accent. She is followed by the first stripper, wearing a dark, sequined, hourglass gown with a slit up the front allowing a chiffon underlining and her legs to peep through. She dances to a live band and strips off the dress as the music changes to reveal a dark, sequined bra and matching briefs with floor-length chiffon panels attached to front and back. She dances in this until another music change when her bra, the chiffon flaps, and her briefs come off to reveal . . . another, smaller, flesh-colored bikini. She dances in it briefly and then exits to be replaced by two comedians who do a brief and painfully unfunny skit. Five more strippers follow (their performances broken by comic interludes). There is little variation in either their perform-ances or their costumes. The consistent elements are: contemporary formal wear as a starting point, a large fringed or tasseled bra and briefs with sheer chiffon flaps as an interim costume, and a tiny "nude" bikini as a finale.

What is evident in this film's portrayal of the 1950s striptease performance is its nineteenth- and early-twentieth-century roots. Though the cross-dressing aspect of Lydia Thompson burlesque was nowhere to be seen, the emphasis on the coyly revealed leg is clear. The "formal wear" sported by the stripteasers in the film features side slits or a front panel through which the legs could be revealed, regardless of whether or not such an open-ing was appropriate to the high fashion of the era. Through its emphasis on the legs, the costume is a direct descendant of that worn by the female per-formers of 1860s burlesque theater and bawdy skirt dancers. The second layer of the 1950s burlesque costume keeps the legs on parade while highlighting the second sartorial influence on striptease: Little Egypt Orientalism. The low-slung waistline and spangled and tasseled over bra of the common 1950s costume reference belly dancing costume–keeping the "exotic" in exotic dancing. The final layer of the 1950s costume refers again to the stage gimmicks

Lili St. Cyr–BUILT MORE LIKE A FASHION MODEL THAN A STRIPTEASER–MANAGED TO PUT HER NAME ON A LINE OF COSMETICS IN THE 1950S.

of the Broadway and burlesque "nude." The flesh-colored netting worn by the 1950s strippers both reveals all and reveals nothing. The vulva is empha-sized by the g-string, but remains fully covered. The breasts are visible and set off with pasties, but are clearly constricted within a transparent covering. 1950s striptease, like 1860s burlesque, would seem to be less about the revelation of the flesh than the suggestion of the revelation.

The striptease of the 1950s was an irresistible phenomenon for the press. *Life, Newsweek, Time,*

Lois Defee WAS 6'4" AND WORTH THE CLIMB. IN THE 1940S AND 1950S, STRIPTEASERS WITH EXCEPTIONAL ATTRIBUTES—SUCH AS HEIGHT OR A LARGE BUST—BECAME MORE AND MORE POPULAR AS NIGHTCLUB ATTRACTIONS.

THE G-STRING WAS THE FINAL FRONTIER OF
STRIPTEASE AND THE 1950S STRIPTEASER MADE
ITS REMOVAL LAST AS LONG AS POSSIBLE. HERE,
Lili St. Cyr WEARS THREE G-STRINGS: A TOP
ONE IN FRILLY CHIFFON, A BASIC BLACK ONE IN
THE MIDDLE, AND A FLESH-TONED NET ONE LAST.
ONE OF ST. CYR'S MOST POPULAR ROUTINES WAS
THE "FLYING G-STRING" IN WHICH HER LAST
UNDERGARMENT WAS ATTACHED TO A PIECE
OF INVISIBLE STAGE WIRE WHICH PULLED THE
G-STRING AWAY JUST AS THE STAGE LIGHTS
BLACKED OUT.

LILI ST. CYR 42

STRIPTEASE IN THE 1950S
ABSORBED ALL OF THE VAUDE-
VILLE GIMMICKS. ANIMAL ACTS
LIVED ON WITH BIG CATS, PAR-
ROTS, AND EVEN DOVES TRAINED
TO ASSIST IN UNDRESSING
STRIPTEASERS.

THE FAN DANCE WAS INVENTED
BY FAITH BACON (OR SO SHE
SAID), POPULARIZED BY SALLY
RAND, AND MADE A STRIPTEASE
STAPLE BY ANY AND ALL DANCERS
WHO COULD AFFORD A LARGE
QUANTITY OF FEATHERS.

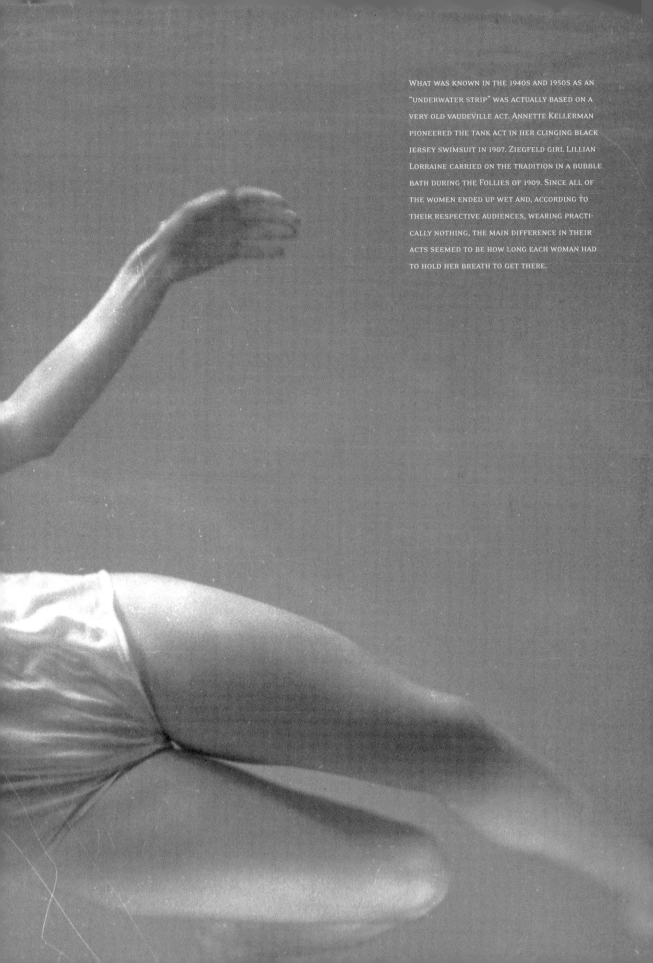

What was known in the 1940s and 1950s as an "underwater strip" was actually based on a very old vaudeville act. Annette Kellerman pioneered the tank act in her clinging black jersey swimsuit in 1907. Ziegfeld girl Lillian Lorraine carried on the tradition in a bubble bath during the Follies of 1909. Since all of the women ended up wet and, according to their respective audiences, wearing practically nothing, the main difference in their acts seemed to be how long each woman had to hold her breath to get there.

PARTY LIKE IT'S 1899: TURN-OF-THE-
CENTURY SHTICK WAS ALIVE AND WELL
IN 1950S STRIPTEASE. THE SPIDER-
WOMAN (BOTTOM) TAKES A PAGE FROM
LOIE FULLER'S BACKLIT SERPENTINE
DANCE WHILE THE EXOTIC DANCER IN
THE HEADBAND ALLUDES TO RUTH ST.
DENIS'S SPIRITUALLY INFLECTED
EGYPTIAN DANCES.

Playboy, and the *New York Times* covered major and minor performers. *Newsweek* reported that burlesque was on the decline but for the mushrooming of exotic dance. According to one article, the number of "ecdysiasts" was estimated at two thousand and had quadrupled since the 1930s. Meanwhile, the number of burlesque houses had shrunk from sixty to twenty-five. Stripteasers could instead be found in the fifty nightclubs in New York City that employed strippers. The article also provided a list of props being used by strippers, including snakes, monkeys, macaws, doves, parakeets, stuffed horses, swimming tanks, and bubble baths; and the names taken by them, such as Carita La Dove-the Cuban Bombshell, Betty de Cue-Duchess of Disrobe, Evelyn West-the $50,000 Treasure Chest Girl, and Melba-The Toast of the Town.

Striptease was even beginning to be the subject of adult education in the 1950s as evidenced by a "field trip" taken by a class from The New School for Social Research to a New Jersey Minsky theater that was covered by both *Time* and the *New York Times Magazine.* The *Time* article takes care to describe the group as "no ordinary Minskyites" and delights in the teacher's discomfort with the performance, narrating that "Teacher Bill Smith . . . became more and more embarrassed. . . . He had forgotten how low burlesque had sunk." Meanwhile, the students are portrayed as interested. In a description of the same event, the *New York Times Magazine* quotes the teacher of the class at length: "'I want to point out,' Smith went on resolutely, 'that burlesque as we know it came into being about—uh—1926 or '27, when the stripper came along. . . . Before that, it was not an integral part of burlesque.'"

But, in fact, the striptease *had* been an integral part of burlesque, and of vaudeville as well. That was what made it a success in the 1950s—it was the last surviving act of a century of populist stage entertainment. Unfortunately, its success in the 1950s would prove to be its downfall. Its popularity required more and more performers, some less talented than others. The gimmicks used by Starr and St. Cyr fell into disuse in favor of simply stripping off the dress. In lieu of the element of amusement provided by the gimmicks and comedy of striptease, clubs offered more intimate contact with the performers. The managers required stripteasers to hustle patrons for drinks and their salaries were reduced to increase their reliance on a cut of the bar profits. By the 1960s, the stage time for a stripteaser was becoming limited as performers were required to spend part of their time in close contact with individual audience members. The distance from which the stripteasers could tease the audience was disappearing. And as striptease was being widely disseminated, it lost its novelty. The cyclical process of shocking innovation followed by mass adaptation followed by new shocking innovation that had characterized the history of striptease was in effect again. The burlesque queens had been done in by vaudeville's various skirt dancers. The skirt dancers had been rendered obsolete by modern dancers Loie Fuller, Isadora Duncan, Ruth St. Denis, and Maud Allan. The modern dancers had been imitated into irrelevance by Ziegfeld's glorified girls. The women of the revues had been outdone and undercut by Gypsy Rose Lee and other Minsky stars. And, finally, the 1950s striptease stars were outstripped as well.

What would replace Starr, Storm, St. Cyr, and their lesser imitators is exemplified by one of the most iconic figures of 1950s culture: Bettie Page. Bettie Page was a contemporary of the 1950s stripteasers. She appeared in the 1950s striptease films *Varietease* and *Teaserama* along with Lili St.

As Hugh Hefner reinvented the sexual ideal through his *Playboy* magazine, the large-breasted stripteaser gave way to a younger, more lithe alternative: the girl next door (who just happened to be naked).

---

opposite: **Bettie Page** was no headliner in 1950s striptease, but she was the most popular pin-up of 1955. And as the decade progressed, those girls in pin-ups were replacing stripteasers as objects of desire.

GYPSY ROSE LEE ONCE QUOTED HER
MOTHER AS SAYING, "NOTHING
WILL EVER TAKE THE PLACE OF
FLESH." THIS WAS AS TRUE IN THE
1950S AS IT HAD BEEN IN THE 1930S.
ALTHOUGH THE IDEAL OF THE
Playboy bunny REPLACED THE
STAR STRIPTEASER, THE AUDIENCE
STILL WANTED THAT BUNNY IN
THE FLESH. PLAYBOY STARTED ITS
OWN CHAIN OF GENTLEMAN'S
CLUBS IN ORDER TO DELIVER.

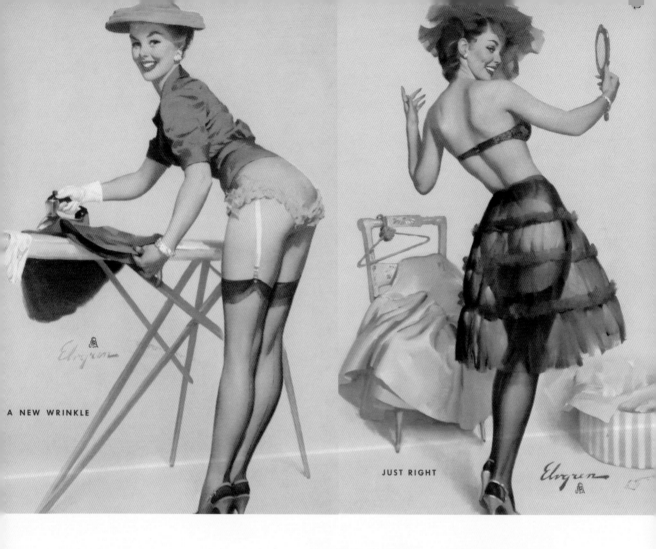

A NEW WRINKLE

JUST RIGHT

above: IN THE 1940S, THE SEXY PIN-UP GIRL BEGAN
AN ASCENT IN AMERICAN POPULAR CULTURE THAT
WOULD CULMINATE IN *Playboy* MAGAZINE. THESE
GIL ELVGREN PIN-UPS, ORIGINALLY DISTRIBUTED AS
PROMOTIONAL MATERIAL BY AN AUTO PARTS SALES-
MAN, ARE THE MISSING LINK BETWEEN VARGAS'S
PAINTINGS OF ZIEGFELD GIRLS AND HUGH HEFNER'S
HEAVILY RETOUCHED CENTERFOLD PLAYMATES.

right: Cabaret WAS A 1950S MAGAZINE DEVOTED TO
STRIPTEASERS AND NIGHTCLUB ENTERTAINMENT.

NOVEMBER 1956 50¢

CABARET
THE ADULT ENTERTAINMENT MAGAZINE

WALTER
WINCHELL:
AMERICA'S TOP
STARMAKER

MASTER OF THE
RISQUE JOKE

HOW TO
MAKE BOSOM
FRIENDS IN
THE ORIENT
By Jennie Lee

BRITAIN'S
NON-STOP
PEEPSHOW

THE SEX LIFE OF A STRIPPER

Cyr and Blaze Starr. She was even friends with Tempest Storm. She was not, however, a striptease headliner. She was a pin-up girl. Her fame (and she didn't consider herself famous in the 1950s) came from the numerous pictures of her on magazine covers, for Irving Klaw's *Movie Star News*, and for camera clubs. Page's picture was so ubiquitous that she was named "Miss Pin-Up Girl of the World" in 1955. The same year, she was made a *Playboy* centerfold. Page's appeal was in her girl-next-door look. That, in combination with her presentation as a picture, not in person, made her a figure of erotic intrigue—she was at once more intimate and more safely removed than the figure of the stripteaser. Bettie Page was the first noticeable star of what would become the next category of sex symbol.

Playboy publisher Hugh Hefner would do the most to promote the girl-next-door pin-up as sexual icon during the 1950s. Like Ziegfeld before him, Hefner positioned himself as a connoisseur of female beauty capable of transforming a beautiful girl into an object of mass adulation. And he would follow Ziegfeld's example in raiding the nightclubs for talent while excluding the nightclub's stripteasers. Hefner's magazine embraced all the elements of the 1950s nightclub: the promotion of cocktail culture, a reverence for jazz music, and an affinity for edgy comedians, but openly mocked stripteasers like Tempest Storm. In the place of those stripteasers, Hefner offered a younger, more lithe alternative. Smiling Bettie Page fit this mold while overtly sexual performers like Blaze Starr did not.

Hefner's *Playboy* magazine covered striptease a little in pictorials like "Paris Hot Spots," "Paris 'Round the World," "Burlesque in Tokyo," "Filming the Folies-Bergère," "Latin Quarter Lovelies," "Minsky in Vegas," and "Les Girls, Les Girls, Les Girls," but the few written articles on 1950s striptease were entirely condescending. One piece was opened with the statement "There was a time when a girl could count on an enthusiastic audience by simply peeling down to her birthday suit. Not so today. The modern male is a jaded animal." The author goes on to recount gimmicks currently in vogue in striptease such as costumed assistants, the use of animals, a bathtub, a g-string rigged to be removed via invisible wire, a trained bird, and underwater stripping. He concludes "All of these clever goings on are designed to make show lounge sex more interesting and, at that, they're pretty successful. Nevertheless, all things considered, we prefer our sex in the bedroom." Another article, about striptease headliner Tempest Storm, takes a similar superior attitude: "Miss Storm is, in the words of her press agent, 'a strip tease recitalist.'" On the whole, the *Playboy* articles portray striptease as laughable in comparison to the actual sex that the *Playboy* reader is assumed to be having (with the girl next door, no doubt).

Hefner's pin-up girls, some of whom had been employed as stripteasers when they were "discovered" but were never advertised as such, replaced the stripteasers as objects of desire over the course of the 1950s. The *Playboy* model's supposed "accessibility" spurred the development of more intimate contact in nightclubs. Gimmicks became archaic. The tease was made obsolete—it was not something the girl next door would do. Although Hefner's presentation of this new sex object was as contrived as Blaze Starr's flaming settee, it became the reigning erotic ideal. And the stripteaser lost her place on the stage. ★

EPILOGUE

Made &

ou Book!

THE WORLD FAMOUS *BOB*

Porn killed stripping... in my day, nudity was so rare—*so special.*

—Blaze Starr, 1989

IT WOULD BE EASY TO WRITE AN EPILOGUE TO THIS HIS-tory decrying the current state of striptease in comparison to a 1950s "golden era." Things have certainly changed enough. 1950s censorship and obscenity laws precluded complete nudity in striptease. Pasties were required, as was the g-string. Now ornate pasties are quaint relics. If the law demands that the nipples be covered, liquid latex is used to cover them and still simulate the flesh. In most cases, however, nipples roam free in strip clubs. And the g-string is no longer the final frontier—it was removed in the late 1960s. And it has never been recovered. Strippers are completely naked now, and that doesn't leave much to build an act around. The revelation of all that flesh *is* the show. Once, a pair of sequined, tasseled pasties was the shorthand representation of the stripper. Now it is a naked girl dancing next to a pole—the almost laughably obvious phallic symbol at the center of what's left of a stage in most strip clubs. Back in the day, strippers had names that were posted on

nightclub marquees. They were famous for their striptease acts. Now, there are no striptease "stars," and the only names that appear on strip club marquees, if the club even has a marquee, are those of touring porn stars.

There's a whole book in what happened to striptease between the 1950s and the present. That book would start with the decline of the star strip-teaser. In the Broadway musical *Damn Yankees,* the character of Lola, a minion of Satan, performs a striptease in order to seduce the protagonist into surrendering his soul. Her act fails to win the protagonist over and the Devil mocks her saying, "your act is tired." Striptease was tired by the end of the 1950s. The cocktail nation that had patronized striptease nightclubs was tired too, and getting a little long in the tooth. As the playboys and their playmates went home to sleep it off in the early 1960s, a new figure appeared: the go-go dancer. They were nubile young things that sprang out of the so-called youth quake of the early 1960s. Not only were they young, they were also markedly slimmer than stripteasers. They didn't have any act other than to dance with joyous smiles on their faces. Go-go dancers were everywhere in the 1960s. They wore mod fashions, mini-skirts, and naturally, go-go boots. They were in the background on platforms as rock bands played on television comedy shows, and down at the local bar. Some of them were volunteers—dancing for fun or to meet the band. Others were paid to be eye candy. Strip club managers were not ones to miss out on a new gimmick. They began hiring and advertising the new dancers, and nightclubs that had featured hot jazz and star stripteasers soon became go-go bars. Although clearly not all go-go dancers performed in strip clubs, they were increasingly sexualized as the decade went on. While the image of the Swinging London go-go girl was relatively innocent, a foil to that was Russ Meyers's portrayal of go-go girl as thrill killer in *Faster Pussycat, Kill, Kill.* As a nameless mass, free of any of the pretensions of stardom, go-go girls were suited to the changing layout of the strip club. They didn't require a stage, they danced in cages, on bars, and on tables, and they were increasingly accessible.

In the mid-1960s, one of the go-go girls at a San Francisco strip club danced in fashion designer Rudi Gernreich's topless bathing suit . . . and didn't get arrested. From that point, the topless trend emerged. Strip clubs began hosting topless lunches and offering topless shoe shines. By the end of the 1960s, bottomless dancers started performing, too. Full nudity remained the order of the day into the 1970s as pornography emerged into the mainstream and made even live sex acts possible in strip clubs. For a period in the 1970s, stripping became only an adjunct to a massive sex industry of which hardcore pornographic films were the centerpiece.

The lines between stripping, prostitution, and other kinds of sex work were briefly blurred.

In the 1980s, a backlash occurred against the more blatant public sex acts in strip clubs and against pornography. Attorney General Edwin Meese prosecuted pornographers and issued a report connecting pornography with violence against women. With pornography somewhat repressed, the strip club emerged again as an independent entity. The 1980s stripper was toned and athletic and often had surgically enhanced breasts. She was distributed across America in "gentleman's" clubs that opened up in mid-size southern and midwestern cities that had previously been free of striptease, except at the back of the carnival midway. The 1980s stripper became a fixture in heavy metal videos and buddy cop movies. As gentleman's clubs proved profitable in Middle America, they multiplied. A mid-size city could contain a Doll House, a Tattletails, *and* a Gold Club. The increased competition engendered the lap dance—a direct correlation developed between the amount of contact with the stripper and the money paid to her. By the 1990s, the lap dance had been choreographed into just another dance move in the stripper's repertoire. Standard rates were set for it—tipping for additional time or contact was an option, as much as the law allowed.

Of course, 1950s stripteasers will tell you that there was some of that sort of thing in their day as well. 1950s New Orleans stripteaser Wild Cherry explains that touring stripteasers who weren't stars were expected to sit with, drink with, and get pawed by audience members. It was a tradition that went back to concert saloons. What really marks the difference between strippers now and stripteasers in the 1950s is that stripteasers used to be stars. They were separated from the audience

opposite: **Scarlette Fever** IS A MEMBER OF THE LOS ANGELES-BASED NEW BURLESQUE TROUPE, VELVET HAMMER.

PERFORMER *Jane Blevin* EXEMPLIFIES THE COMMITMENT TO TRADITION IN NEW BURLESQUE. SHE TRAINED WITH 1950S STRIPTEASER KITTY WEST TO BECOME EVANGELINE THE OYSTER GIRL—AN ATTRACTION IN BURLESQUE AND CARNIVALS SINCE THE TURN OF THE CENTURY.

not only by a stage, but by an aura of celebrity as well. Strippers after the 1950s were, ideally, real girls. Not exactly the girl next door, but real girls nonetheless. It was an illusion for the most part, but one that strip club managers struggled to maintain. The go-go girls who populated the 1960s strip clubs were there to suggest that the fresh young things men had seen on television behind the pop band had just happened by the club and had to dance. Russ Meyers introduces his go-go dancers in *Faster Pussycat, Kill, Kill* with the unlikely aside that they were "secretaries by day," wishful thinking, perhaps, for the film's audience— the truth was that Meyers recruited his actresses from strip clubs, not the secretarial pool. Still, Meyers wanted to maintain the idea that they were accessible. The wet t-shirt contest served a similar function in the 1970s strip club. The idea was that any local woman could enter, get sprayed down, and win the contest. The appeal of this was that the women there to be ogled weren't professionals; they were the girls next door. The only problem with this is that strippers were often the main competitors in the contests. The myth of stripper as good girl gone wild is maintained even today with amateur nights at strip clubs and strippers who claim to be "working their way through college." That's not to say that some women performing on amateur nights aren't amateurs or that no one's ever worked her way through college stripping, it's just that the idea is part of what strip club managers are selling.

One thing that is certain is that the stripper is as much a figure of intrigue to the press and the public as the stripteaser. Strippers are the subjects of quasi-documentary shows on cable television. They are the eye candy in the background, and sometimes the foreground, of music videos. Former stripper Anna Nicole Smith has her own TV show. Former stripper Lily Burana is the author of a successful memoir, *Strip City,* in which she recounts her life story and her own "farewell tour" of strip clubs that she undertook before getting married. There are "stripper-cize" classes being taught at fitness centers in New York City and Los Angeles and a striptease class is even offered at seven sister school Mount Holyoke. Stripping isn't striptease, but it is still an entertainment that holds a lot of people's interest in America. It's just that now the interest is in the stripper as a type, not as a specific person—the result of decades of establishing the stripper as an ordinary girl, not a celebrity.

Even as stripping is big business in America, striptease is far from a lost art. In the past few years, a movement dubbed the New Burlesque has been taking place in nightclubs, gay bars, and swing dance clubs in cities such as New York City, San Francisco, New Orleans, Los Angeles, Denver, Baltimore, and Seattle. Performers in the New Burlesque are campy, funny, and sexy. Their shows are intended to draw women as well as men to the audience. One of the stars of the New Burlesque scene is The World Famous *BOB*, who looks like a plus-size Marilyn Monroe. At 5'10", *BOB* started out performing in gay clubs as a "female female impersonator." Her acts include making a drink using her breasts to agitate the martini shaker and topless aerobics performed to the tune of AC/DC's "You Shook Me All Night Long" while eating a cheeseburger. *BOB*'s work is at once a send-up of and a tribute to the extreme version of femininity presented by 1950s stripteasers. Another New Burlesque pioneer is Dirty Martini who performs traditional fan dances and balloon dances. Martini started out a classically trained dancer challenged by a body unsuited to ballet. She said she discovered

THE EMPHATICALLY CURVY LADIES IN THIS 2001 VELVET HAMMER POSTER BY ARTIST THE PIZZ ARE REMINISCENT OF THE CARTOON STRIPTEASERS WHO ONCE GRACED THE BACK PAGES OF THE 1950S GIRLIE MAGAZINE *Cabaret.*

following spread: IN 2002, THE SECOND ANNUAL TEASE-O-RAMA CONFERENCE WAS HELD IN SAN FRANCISCO. BILLED AS A "SULTRY, SIZZLIN' CONVENTION OF BURLESQUE AND DANCE," IT BROUGHT TOGETHER NEW BURLESQUE PERFORMERS FROM ACROSS THE COUNTRY. ***Dirty Martini*** WAS ONE OF THE FEATURED PERFORMERS AND THESE PHOTOS SHOW HER CAMPING IT UP WITH HER BALLOON DANCE.

The Pontani Sisters
BRING BACK THE OLDEST
STYLE OF BURLESQUE BY
NEVER GOING DOWN TO
LESS THAN THEIR WELL-
DECORATED BIKINIS.

in burlesque a style of dance that was designed for her generous proportions. Martini's performances are both revival and revision. Her balloon dance, where she "strips" by using a cigarette to pop off a costume made of pink balloons until she's down to pasties and a g-string, is a traditional 1950s number from the ankles up—her twist is that she performs the dance en point in her ballet shoes, pirouetting and leaping her way across the stage. Martini also does a naughty nurse number, but replaces the traditional nurse's costume with an aqua latex version by fetish designer The Baroness. Martini and *BOB* are top-drawing names in the New York City circuit of nightclubs including The Slipper Room, Suite 16, The VaVaVoom Room, and Joe's Pub. They also perform in the burlesque revival show Kaplan's World Famous Burlesque, based in Coney Island. Neither has ever been a stripper, but they revere striptease.

In Los Angeles, New Burlesque is exemplified by Dita von Teese and Catherine D'lish. Teese is a Bettie Page fan and got her start performing by dressing as Page in look-alike contests. She has also posed as a model in high-end fetish magazines and in *Playboy's Book of Lingerie.* D'Lish has been in numerous "Miss Nude" competitions. They often perform together and specialize in big produc-tion numbers that would make Lili St. Cyr proud. D'Lish performs one elaborately costumed act where she starts out in a sequined gown, strips to under-clothes with a feather-trimmed robe, and then strips to a g-string in order to bathe in a giant cham-pagne glass. Teese and D'Lish perform for the Velvet Hammer in Los Angeles, which is known for the most professionally polished and hard-bodied ver-sion of New Burlesque. D'Lish is an example of a "real" stripper who has found a creative outlet in New Burlesque.

This same overlap between stripping and New Burlesque can be found among some performers in the San Francisco and New Orleans scenes. San Francisco acts run the gamut from the go-go danc-ing Devil-Ettes to traditional stripteasers Dane's Dames to troupes that feature dancers, singers, and full bands. The San Francisco scene developed both from the city's history as a refuge for burlesque, striptease, and stripping, and from the swing craze of the mid-1990s. The interest in swing music and the culture surrounding it created a venue for New Burlesque performers alongside swing revival bands. The New Orleans burlesque troupe the Southern Jeza-belles similarly trades on New Orleans's reputation as a mecca for strippers, using it to draw the city's tourist traffic to shows.

The increasing success of the New Burlesque suggests the possibility that in fifty years time, the live sex acts of the 1970s, and the lap dances of the 1980s and 1990s may only be remembered as a prelude to another era of classic striptease. Currently the history of striptease has come full circle. Strippers find themselves in the place of the nineteenth-century honky-tonk waitresses—"guz-zling bad tea and getting pawed." Of course, those waitresses were among the ones who started it all. They soon became the skirt dancers, modern dancers, glorified girls, and, eventually, the stript-easers. After a wave of success in the 1920s and 1930s, the striptease almost died in the 1940s. After years of disrepute and censorship in the seedier nightclubs and on dusty carnival midways, in the 1950s it made a triumphant return to the mainstream of American entertainment. If New Burlesque performers likewise find an expanded audience, that cycle will, no doubt, repeat itself. The history of striptease teaches nothing if not that there is always something more to be revealed. ☆

SELECTED BIBLIOGRAPHY

ALEXANDER, H. M. *Strip Tease: The Vanished Art of Burlesque.* New York: Knight Publishers, 1938.

ALLEN, ROBERT C. *Horrible Prettiness: Burlesque and American Culture.* Chapel Hill, North Carolina: University of North Carolina Press, 1991.

CARTER, ALISON. *Underwear: The Fashion History.* London: B. T. Batsford Ltd., 1992.

CHERNIASKY, FELIX. *The Salome Dancer: The Life and Times of Maud Allan.* Toronto, Ontario: McClelland & Stewart, Inc., 1991.

CORIO, ANN WITH JOSEPH DIMONA. *This Was Burlesque.* New York: Madison Square Press/Grosset & Dunlap, 1968.

CURRENT, RICHARD NELSON AND MARCIA EWING CURRENT. *Loie Fuller: Goddess of Light.* Boston: Northeastern University Press, 1997.

DERVAL, PAUL. *Folies-Bergère.* New York: E. P. Dutton & Co., Inc., 1955.

DIJKSTRA, BRAM. *Idols of Perversity: Fantasies of Feminine Evil in Fin-de-Siècle Culture.* New York: Oxford University Press, 1986.

EWING, ELIZABETH. *Dress and Undress: A History of Women's Underwear.* London: B. T. Batsford Ltd., 1989.

FIELDS, ARMOND AND L. MARC FIELDS. *From the Bowery to Broadway: Lew Fields and the Roots of American Popular Theater.* New York: Oxford University Press, 1993.

FOSTER, RICHARD. *The Real Bettie Page: The Truth About the Queen of the Pinups.* New York: Citadel Press, 1997.

FOUCAULT, MICHEL. *The History of Sexuality, Volume 1: An Introduction.* Translated by Robert Hurley. New York: Pantheon-Random, 1978.

GOLD, ARTHUR AND ROBERT FIZDALE. *The Divine Sarah: A Life of Sarah Bernhardt.* 2nd ed. New York: Vintage Books, 1992.

GOLDEN, EVE. *Anna Held and the Birth of Ziegfeld's Broadway.* Lexington, Kentucky: The University Press of Kentucky, 2000.

HARRIS, NEIL. *Humbug: The Art of P. T. Barnum.* Phoenix Edition, 1981. Chicago: The University of Chicago Press, 1973.

HOARE, PHILIP. *Wilde's Last Stand: Decadence, Conspiracy and the First World War.* London: Gerald Duckworth & Co. Ltd., 1997.

JARRET, LUCINDA. *Stripping in Time: A History of Erotic Dancing.* London: Pandora-Harper, 1977.

LAURIE, JOE JR. *Vaudeville: From the Honky-Tonks to the Palace.* New York: Henry Holt and Company, 1953.

LEE, GYPSY ROSE. *Gypsy.* Berkeley, California: Frog, Ltd., 1957.

LESLIE, PETER. *A Hard Act To Follow: A Music Hall Review.* New York & London: Paddington Press, Ltd., 1978.

LEWIS, ARTHUR H. *La Belle Otero.* New York: Trident Press, 1967.

MACDOUGALL, ALLAN ROSS. *Isadora: A Revolutionary in Art and Love.* New York: Thomas Nelson & Sons, 1960.

MARIEL, PIERRE AND JEAN TROCHER. *Paris Cancan.* Trans. Stephanie & Richard Sutton. London: Charles Skilton Ltd., 1961.

MINSKY, MORTON. *Minsky's Burlesque.* New York: Arbor, 1986.

MIZEJEWSKI, LINDA. *Ziegfeld Girl: Image and Icon in Culture and Cinema.* Durham & London: Duke University Press, 1999.

PARKER, DEREK AND JULIA PARKER. *The Natural History of the Chorus Girl.* Indianapolis & New York: Bobbs-Merrill, 1975.

SHELTON, SUZANNE. *Divine Dancer: A Biography of Ruth St. Denis.* New York: Doubleday & Company, Inc., 1981.

SOBEL, BERNARD. *Burleycue: An Underground History of Burlesque Days.* New York: Farrar & Rinehart Inc., 1931.

_____. *A Pictorial History of Burlesque.* New York: Bonanza Books, 1956.

STARR, BLAZE AND HUEY PERRY. *Blaze Starr: My Life as Told to Huey Perry.* Warner Paperback Library Edition. New York: Praeger Publishers, Inc., 1975.

STENCELL, A. W. *Girl Show: Into the Canvas World of Bump and Grind.* Toronto: ECW Press, 1999.

STORM, TEMPEST. *The Lady Is A Vamp.* Atlanta: Peachtree Publishers, Ltd., 1987.

ZEIDMAN, IRVING. *The American Burlesque Show.* New York: Hawthorn Books, Inc., 1967.

ZIEGFELD, RICHARD AND PAULETTE. *The Ziegfeld Touch: The Life and Times of Florenz Ziegfeld Jr.* New York: Harry N. Abrams, Inc., 1993.

Page numbers in *italics* refer to illustrations

PHOTOGRAPH AND ILLUSTRATION CREDITS

MICHAEL COGLIANTRY PHOTOGRAPHY: page 168; © CORBIS: pages 4–5; CULVER PICTURES: pages 2–3, 12, 15, 16 (top right), 33 (left), 35 (bottom), 40 (right), 43, 46 (right), 70–71, 76, 78 (top), 80, 83 (top left), 84 (bottom), 88 (left), 96–97, 106, 109, 112–113, 120, 129, 136, 137, 142, and 146; THE DAYTON ART INSTITUTE: page 49. Jean-Léon Gérôme (1824–1904) French. *Dance of the Almeh,* 1863. Oil on wood panel, 19 3/4 x 32 inches. The Dayton Art Institute / Gift of Mr. Robert Badenhop, 1951.15; PHOTOGRAPH BY JEFF GARDNER: pages 158–159; COLLECTION JESSICA GLASSCOCK: pages 6–7, 124 (both), 126 (all 3), 127 (all 3), and 156 (all 3); COLLECTION KEN GLICKFELD: pages 16 (top left), 22, 24 (both), 29 (both), 30 (right), 33 (right), 34 (both), 50 (both), 67 (top left), 83 (bottom), 84 (top), 95, and 134; PHOTOGRAPHS BY LAURA HERBERT: pages 166–167; HULTON | ARCHIVE BY GETTY IMAGES: pages 94, 116–117, 148–149, and 154–155; LIBRARY OF CONGRESS, PRINTS AND PHOTOGRAPHS DIVISION, ARNOLD GENTHE COLLECTION: NEGATIVES AND TRANSPARENCIES: pages 64 (top) [LC-G401-Bn-9107], 64 (bottom) [LC-G401-T-1476-002], 67 (bottom) [LC-G39-T-0301-G-040]; LIBRARY OF CONGRESS, PRINTS AND PHOTOGRAPHS DIVISION: pages 13 [LC-USZC4-1705], 16 (bottom) [LC-USZC4-5379], 26 [LC-USZC4-1716], 27 (left) [LC-USZC4-1703], 27 (right) [LC-USZC4-1717], 42 [LC-USZ62-109526], 46 (left) [LC-USZ62-110495], 47 (top) [LC-USZ62-95564], 47 (bottom) [LC-USZ62-21442], 52 [LC-USZ62-105070], 55 [LC-USZ62-102130], 56 [LC-USZ62-90930], 57 [LC-USZ62-9093], 68 [LC-USZ61 1045], 74 [LC-USZC4-5163], and 75 [LC-USZ6-448]; PHOTOGRAPHS BY SCOTT LINDGREN: pages 162–163; MOVIE STAR NEWS: pages 9 (all 4), 139 (all 4), 140, 143, 144–145, and 152; NEW YORK DAILY NEWS: page 118; JOHN PEDIN/NEW YORK DAILY NEWS: pages 132–133; BILLY ROSE THEATRE COLLECTION, THE NEW YORK PUBLIC LIBRARY FOR THE PERFORMING ARTS, ASTOR, LENOX AND TILDEN FOUNDATIONS: pages 25, 30 (left), 39, 40 (left), 62–63, 77, 78 (bottom), 100–101, 107, 110, and 114; JEROME ROBBINS DANCE DIVISION, THE NEW YORK PUBLIC LIBRARY FOR THE PERFORMING ARTS, ASTOR, LENOX AND TILDEN FOUNDATIONS: pages 11, 18, 23, 32, 35 (top), 36, 37, 38, 58, 59, 60 (both), 67 (top right), 83 (top right), 87, 88 (right), 90, 91, 103, 128, and 131; ARTWORK BY THE PIZZ. PRINTED BY HARPOON AT DRAG PUNK INDUSTRIES: page 165; UNIVERSITY PRINT COLLECTION, UCR/CALIFORNIA MUSEUM OF PHOTOGRAPHY: pages 10, 147, 150 (both), and 153.

Acknowledgments go . . .

To my mother, Terry Rodriguez, who convinced me I could do anything; to my father, Mace Glasscock, who made me rewrite everything; to Louise Melling and Catherine Weiss, who made me realize I'd rather eat glass than become a lawyer; to Emily Sparrow, who was the best American history teacher ever; to Effie Cannon, who made me a better writer even as I called her vile names under my breath; to Lourdes Font, who is as fine a professor as she is a disher of Oscar gowns; to the librarians, pages, and picture collection managers of the New York Public Library's Library for the Performing Arts, who could not possibly get paid enough; to Deborah Aaronson, who was an endlessly patient editor; to Brankica Kovrlija, who made room even for my unwieldy chapter titles in her wonderful book design; and to Jack from the Palace Bar for "From Gaslight to Spotlight."

EDITOR ☆ *Deborah Aaronson*
DESIGNER ☆ *Brankica Kovrlija*
PRODUCTION MANAGER ☆ *Justine Keefe*

LIBRARY OF CONGRESS CATALOGING-IN-PUBLICATION DATA

Glasscock, Jessica.
  Striptease : from gaslight to spotlight / Jessica Glasscock.
    p. cm.
Includes bibliographical references and index.
  ISBN 0-8109-4544-4
  1. Striptease—United States—History. 2. Sex in dance—United
States. 3. Striptease—Social aspects. I. Title.

  PN1949.S7G57 2003
  792.7'0973—dc21
                                2003003815

PRINTED AND BOUND IN CHINA

10 9 8 7 6 5 4 3 2 1

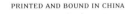

HARRY N. ABRAMS, INC.
100 Fifth Avenue
New York, N.Y. 10011
www.abramsbooks.com

Abrams is a subsidiary of
 LA MARTINIÈRE
              G R O U P E

front and back endpapers: PAGES FROM *Cabaret* MAGAZINE, NOVEMBER 1956.
pages 2-3: THE REAL DEAL: A MINSKY STRIPTEASER, C. 1937.
pages 4-5: JACK RUBY STRIPPERS.

THE SEX LIFE OF A STRIPPER

Married six times, burlesque beauty Nudema reveals some rules of wedded bliss that don't fit rulebooks, such as love is impossible without money

By Henry Durling

IN THE chaotic Bohemian tangle of a night club stripper's existence, nothing is ever quite so complicated—and so often fouled up—as her sex life. Somehow the girls who make it all so attractive and simple on stage seem to have the most difficulty of anyone in grasping for themselves offstage the joys which they hint so alluringly of to their audiences.

This is partly because the girls who know so well what their audiences want, seldom know what they themselves want, or else they know too well, and never find it. It is also because the topsy-turvy timing of their lives, with barely enough room in 24 hours for sleep, grooming, travel and work, leaves little opportunity for settling into a domestic routine.

They glitter through hundreds of romances, offstage and on, laughing and reveling in the champagne glamour of their stardom, but all are on the lookout for the one man who can offer them the snug harbor of married bliss and masculine protection.

One such—perhaps the most experienced and indefatigable of them all—is a pert, brown-eyed seductress called Nudema, a charming much-married girl, sometimes a redhead, sometimes a brunette, and very occasionally a blonde, who never gives up hope.

For Nudema, who was born Pat Murphy, the daughter of an Army officer at Ft. Knox, Ky., the search for love and happiness in her sex life has swept her through 25 engagements and no less than six marriages in her 26 years and she's still looking.

"Marrige," says the fiery Nudema, "is a habit which, unfortunately, I have never had an opportunity to develop with any of my husbands."

As a result, each has regretfully but inevitably been consigned to her scrapbook, and the marriage to the scrapheap. But these experiences have not embittered Nudema. She is, if anything, grateful for the oppor-

PATTING HIPS, Nudema calls attention to well-rounded personality assets at beginning of act which includes champagne bath and donning of filmy negligees before final curtain drops.